ED SHEERAN

THIS IS A CARLTON BOOK

Published by Carlton Books Limited
20 Mortimer Street
London W1T 3JW

A CIP catalogue for this book is available from the
British Library.

ISBN 978-1-78739-048-5

Editor: Chris Mitchell
Design Manager: Russell Knowles
Designer: James Pople
Picture Research: Paul Langan
Production Coordinator: Yael Steinitz

10 9 8 7 6 5 4 3 2 1

ED SHEERAN

Writing Out Loud

CAROLINE SULLIVAN

CARLTON
BOOKS

CONTENTS

CHAPTER ONE
2011 // ALBUM: +

CHAPTER TWO
2014 // ALBUM: X

CHAPTER THREE
2017 // ALBUM: ÷

INTRODUCTION

ED SHEERAN HAS REASON TO REMEMBER 16 MARCH 2017. THAT WAS THE DAY THAT ALL 16 TRACKS FROM HIS THIRD ALBUM, ÷ (DIVIDE), ENTERED THE UK TOP 20 SINGLES CHART. IT HAD NEVER HAPPENED BEFORE AND, THANKS TO A HASTY REJIGGING OF THE RULES, IT WILL NEVER HAPPEN AGAIN. THAT WILL BE ONE FOR SHEERAN TO TELL HIS GRANDCHILDREN.

If anyone needed convincing that the man from Framlingham, Suffolk was the predominant singer-songwriter of the decade, that should have done it. But, in his low-key, self-deprecating way, Sheeran had broken a dozen records before that. The first singer to play Wembley Stadium solo? That was him, for three nights in 2015. The artist who logged the most Spotify streams in one day? Also him (68 million on 3 March 2017, the day of ÷'s release). Fastest-selling album in the UK by a male artist? Sheeran again (÷ clocked up 672,000 sales in its first week). And that was on top of his previous two album's feats: x (Multiply) was the top-selling album of 2014 and second-best seller of 2015, and his 2011 debut, + (Plus), knocked Adele's unassailable 21 off the Number 1 spot in its week of release.

   The remarkable thing is that Sheeran accomplished all this by being the antithesis of a 2010s pop star. Though he came of age in the era of social media – which was how early fans spread the word about him – he has the hallmarks of an earlier generation of songwriters. When he started writing as a teenager, his influences were decidedly mid-twentieth century; apart from Damien Rice and Eminem, he loved The Beatles, Van Morrison, Derek and the Dominos and Dylan. Remarkably for someone who was born in 1991, one of his favourite songs was the Dominos' "Layla", which came out 20 years before his birth. Dominos main-man Eric Clapton made him want to learn guitar, he told *Rolling Stone* in 2015. Sheeran saw him play "Layla" on TV at the Queen's Golden Jubilee and was mesmerised. "Of course, no one plays like Clapton, least of all me."

By 13, Sheeran was writing and releasing his own home-burned CDs and, by 16, he was playing gigs. He was tireless, setting up his guitar and amp at pubs, local fêtes and open-mic nights, while sending his music to record companies, hoping that one would decide that what its roster needed was a singer-songwriter who fused folk and hip hop. The gigs were a grind – the same venues, same promoters and same audiences, over and over again – and he was turned down by every label. They did have two pieces of advice for him, however: ditch the loop pedal – the piece of equipment that enables him to construct layers of sound onstage – and cut out the rap bits because "nobody wants to see a ginger, white guy rapping."

   His songwriting style began to develop then, and has remained rooted in storytelling and melody. He was a typical "Noughties" kid, loving hip hop and its UK-born offshoot, grime, and his delivery is influenced by their lyrical flow. In contrast to their emphasis on beats, though, Sheeran's songs err on the side of big, anthemic choruses. Beats play a role in his music and the loop station helps to make the whole thing sound fleshier but he writes with an emphasis on melody.

   He has a traditional song-man's dexterity, with hook-lines, but he's not retro; he's immersed in twenty-first-century pop and has worked with some of the biggest names in grime and dance music, including Pharrell, The Weeknd and Wiley. Desert Island Discs presenter Kirsty Young summed up his selling point when he appeared as a castaway in 2017: he "bridges the gap between Dylan and Eminem." That's as good a way as any to put it.

Caroline Sullivan, 2018

CHAPTER ONE

2011 // ALBUM: +

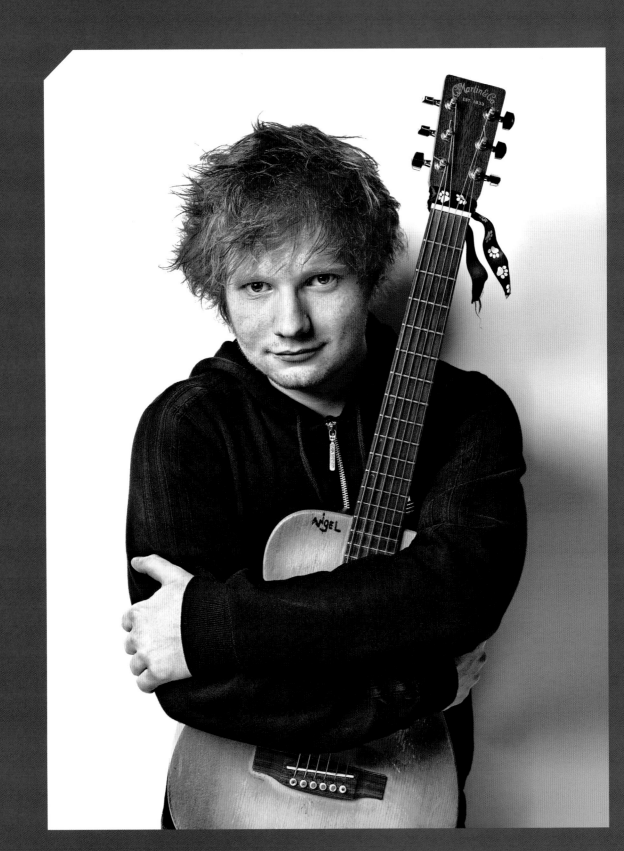

SHEERAN RELEASED SEVERAL EPS INDEPENDENTLY BEFORE JOINING THE ASYLUM RECORDS ROSTER IN EARLY 2011, SIGNING THE CONTRACT AT HIS PARENTS' KITCHEN TABLE SHORTLY BEFORE HIS 20TH BIRTHDAY. HE CAME TO THE LABEL'S ATTENTION WHEN HE SUPPORTED THE BRIEFLY SUCCESSFUL SINGER/RAPPER JUST JACK ON TOUR AND, SUBSEQUENTLY, SELF-RELEASED *NO 5 COLLABORATIONS PROJECT*, AN EP FEATURING DUETS WITH GRIME STARS INCLUDING WILEY AND GHETTS. WHEN IT UNEXPECTEDLY REACHED NUMBER 1 IN THE ITUNES CHART, "THE PHONE CALLS STARTED COMING THICK AND FAST," HIS MANAGER, STUART CAMP, TOLD MUSIC BUSINESS WORLDWIDE. IF *NO 5 COLLABORATIONS PROJECT* HAD BEEN A RELATIVELY LOW-KEY INTRODUCTION TO A PRODIGIOUS TALENT, SHEERAN'S DEBUT ALBUM WAS WHERE HE PROPERLY SET OUT HIS STALL.

Relentless touring had been a proving ground, letting him road-test material and hone his act. By the time he began work on the album he'd devised a sound of his own. Producer Jake Gosling, who had his first success with Wiley in 2008, co-wrote seven tracks on + and co-produced all but "Kiss Me". Between them, they made a record that played up Sheeran's pensive vocals and acoustic guitar – so far, so singer-songwriterly – but also jammed them up against hip-hop rhythms. The fusion gave the songs extra oomph: there were hundreds of acoustic-based songwriters who could string notes into listenable songs but hardly any who used beats and percussion for texture. The result was music that was identifiably pop, yet several measures removed from the pop mainstream.

Sheeran modelled himself on two acts in particular: the English folk/beatbox duo Nizlopi, for whom he once worked as a guitar tech, and Damien Rice, Irish purveyor of raw balladry.

"I knew exactly how I wanted every single song to sound, so each one only took about a day to do," he told the *Daily Mirror* in September 2011, the week before + was released. "I wanted the same sound to go through the album, which I think we achieved."

That they did. And it was fresh and grabby enough to top the charts in five countries, reach the Top 10 in five more and, intriguingly, hit Number 1 in the American folk chart.

The orange album sleeve, by the way, is orange for a reason. Sheeran had spent a lifetime pretending to laugh at ginger jokes, even telling them himself so he could get them out of the way before someone else did. The orange cover, with its tight close-up of Sheeran's face, is his "ginger-in-your-face" moment – the first of many.

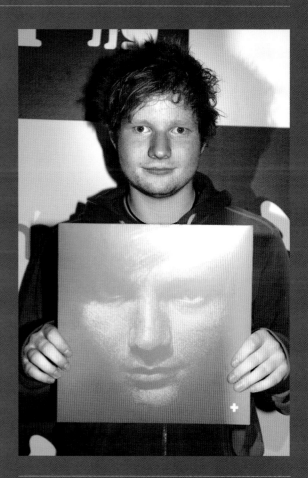

OPPOSITE: With his Little Martin guitar in a 2011 promotional shoot.

ABOVE: Signing copies of + for fans at HMV in Manchester's Arndale Centre, 2011.

THE A TEAM

Unless you were an early adopter, your first exposure to Sheeran probably came in the form of his debut single, "The A Team". It appeared three months ahead of + and was, by anyone's standards, a challenging track to release as the first taste of a new artist. Written by Sheeran alone, with Gosling on production, it tackled three thorny subjects: homelessness, drug addiction and street prostitution.

As pop subject matter, it took up the story where the Arctic Monkeys left off on their 2006 single "When the Sun Goes Down". The black-and-white video that accompanied "The A Team" is also a sort of continuation, with the action transferred from the Monkeys' bleak Sheffield to Sheeran's adopted London.

But Sheeran's lyrics go in a different direction, forensically focusing on the girl at the centre of the song. She was a real person and "Angel", the name in the lyrics, was her real name, though Sheeran changed some of the other details. He met her at a 2009 Christmas gig for the homelessness charity Crisis, where he'd been booked to play a set of cover versions ("She was a big Guns N' Roses fan, so I played 'Sweet Child o' Mine'").

Sheeran was told that, once Crisis closed its Christmas respite centre, Angel would be back on the streets, working as a prostitute to feed her crack addiction. "I was only eighteen at the time and [her story] really affected me," Sheeran said in 2012. He found himself unable to stop thinking about her when he got back to his student flat in Guildford, Surrey, where he was enrolled on a course at the Academy of Contemporary Music.

There's almost nothing to it, other than his breathy vocal, subtle electronics and an acoustic guitar, which he hits with his hand to create a beat. The understatement was deliberate, as was the fact that the track never specifies what drug Angel is using, though the video makes it pretty clear. The clip is dominated by actress Selina McDonald as Angel; Sheeran himself

"I'VE MADE A SONG ABOUT A HOMELESS PROSTITUTE THAT WAS GETTING PLAYED ON A-LIST RADIO. IN TWO WEEKS, I'D SOLD 200,000 COPIES."

ED SHEERAN

LEFT: He's in the Class A Team shirt – HMV, Manchester.

BELOW: With a vinyl copy of "The A Team" at a signing at Fopp Records, London, 2011.

makes a single fleeting appearance in a scene where he buys a copy of the *Big Issue* from her. Filmed for free by one of his friends, the only expense was £20 for fishnet stockings and a crack pipe.

"I didn't really expect it to take off with 'The A Team'" because of what it's about," he said later. But it did. He told the *Sun* later, "I've made a song about a homeless prostitute that was getting played on A-list radio. In two weeks, I'd sold 200,000 copies."

Those early sales are attributable to the silvery delicacy of the tune – it was entirely possible to bask in his silky, enveloping voice and not take in the darkness of the lyrics. There are three remixes, including a reggae take by Shy FX and a hazy dubstep version by Koan Sound. The latter, with its floating vocals, almost mimics the effect of the Class-A drug of the title.

For an introductory shot across the bows, "The A Team" was more successful than Sheeran had dared hope. It sold over 1 million copies in the UK, 2.3 million in America, 420,000 in Australia and another half a million around the rest of the world. Despite a *Guardian* reviewer deciding it was "essentially Phil Collins's 'Another Day in Paradise' for the Moshi Monsters generation," it was the top debut single of 2011 in the UK and was nominated for multiple awards, including a Grammy, a Brit and an Ivor Novello.

He took home only the Ivor, for Best Song Musically and Lyrically, but it was a significant win; the award was decided by songwriters, rather than the industry honchos who normally preside over these things. To have an Ivor trophy decorating his mantelpiece at such an early stage affirmed Sheeran's talent and fulfilled the expectations of those around him – not least his voluble fanbase, the Sheerios.

And there *was* a real-life mantelpiece. At the 2012 Brit Awards, where he was nominated for four gongs and won two (British Breakthrough and British Solo Male), he mused that he had space at home for a statuette or three. "I have a mantelpiece – it hasn't got anything on it. So, yeah, stuff will go on that."

DRUNK

The second track (and fourth single) from + was a Gosling/Sheeran co-write, inspired by Sheeran's experience on a UK tour with London rapper Example in 2010. Example was very much on the way up then and Sheeran was lucky to have got on to the tour as support act. Although he ruled out any joint writing projects with Example, feeling their musical styles didn't gel, they became such close friends that the rapper called him "my little brother". When Sheeran reached the top tier a few years later, Example supported him at his first Wembley Stadium stint.

A week after the Example tour, Sheeran went into the studio with the idea for "Drunk" percolating in his head. While on the road, he'd discovered a new brand of squash, "like Sunny D or something like that," he told *Pop Counterculture* magazine. "If you put vodka in that, you don't really taste the vodka." But isn't tasting it the whole point? Apparently not. Sheeran had been teetotal for a period, requesting only Robinson's peach-flavoured Fruit & Barley squash on his touring rider and, now that he was drinking again, it seems that he hadn't yet redeveloped his palate. At a gig in Glasgow, he put away a fair bit of vodka-squash "and the night kind of disappeared along with it. I woke up on the right side of the wrong bed and missed the tour bus."

Drunkenness also provided material for other + tracks, the most striking being "Wake Me Up", where it's employed as a measure of compatibility. He notes approvingly that his love interest matches him drink for drink, and the icing on the cake is that she loves *Shrek* as much as he does.

If "Drunk" was inspired by a misspent night, it had turned into a break-up song by the time he recorded it. As with "The A Team", the lyrics were finely wrought and believable. His girlfriend has left and he's brooding about her – and, being Sheeran, he finds as much misery in the tiny things as in the big stuff. Now

OPPOSITE: Fans look on as Sheeran shops at Legoland, Carlsbad, California in February 2013.

ABOVE: Example and his "little brother", who had just won the Breakthrough Artist trophy at the 2011 Q Awards in London.

" I DON'T MAKE MUSIC FOR CRITICS. "

ED SHEERAN

that she's gone, he has no one to spend weekends with and just thinking of being alone in their cold flat – she turned off the heating as a final gesture – almost brings him to tears.

Who can't relate? In contrast to the words, though, the amiable, skiffle-hop arrangement is as jaunty as you like. Sheeran has a knack for binding up daggers of emotion in soft-textured wrapping, his voice lending itself to creamy understatement, rather than abrasiveness. (Even during his forays into rapping, he's not quite Tupac. A valiant display of his freestyling skills can be found on YouTube: he and his MC friend Devlin had an impromptu rap battle backstage at Sheffield Academy in 2010, which established that Sheeran is deft but lacks the vocal heft to really make you sit up and listen.)

For all "Drunk"'s merits as a song, where it really comes into its own is in the video, which was directed by Iranian-American filmmaker Saman Kesh. The ex-girlfriend is played by Sheeran's actual girlfriend at the time, the Scottish pop singer Nina Nesbitt, and the co-starring role went to a cat. Having been dumped by text message even as he was waiting for his girl at Paddington Station, Sheeran stumbles home and has the first of many beers, vodkas and shots.

It turns out that not only can his cat speak but he's also partial to a drink himself. "Hey, Ed! Pass that beer over," he commands and, once they're both soused, he tries to ease Ed's heartache. They play video games, go to the pub and then have a house party, where the cat attempts to introduce Sheeran to the prettiest girl in the room.

When he awakes the next morning, he discovers that the party and the talking cat were all a dream, and he has nothing to show for it but a hangover.

ABOVE: Scottish songwriter Nina Nesbitt, whom he dated in 2011.

OPPOSITE: Photoshoot at Asylum Records, Kensington, London in July 2011.

U.N.I.

If there's one thing Sheeran has capitalised on, it's his "every-bloke" appeal. His songs are relatable because they're believable; brimming with details that everyone recognises. And, despite having been a teenager when he wrote most of +, his music speaks not only to his own age-group but also to his parents'.

In the eyes of rock critics, an artist with multi-generational appeal is deeply unhip, as Sheeran himself has acknowledged: "As I'm aware, I'm not the most critically acclaimed artist out there," he said on Facebook in 2017. But it also means that a much larger audience hears the music.

In the case of "U.N.I.", the older segment of his fanbase would have been nodding reminiscently as Sheeran adroitly captured the mingled excitement and despair of a couple splitting up because one of them is off to university. And his younger fans also would also understand because Sheeran resembled their older brother who'd gone off to college.

That Sheeran never actually went to university is briefly touched on in this pretty, semi-acoustic track. As he explains it, his girlfriend lives in halls of residence, while he spends his life touring. (It's worth mentioning that he was one of only two people in

ABOVE: It makes a change from the hoodie: receiving an honorary degree from Suffolk university for his outstanding contribution to music, October 2015.

OPPOSITE: Meeting the Queen (and Kylie Minogue) at Buckingham Palace after the Diamond Jubilee Concert, June 2012.

"I DON'T REALLY LOOK LIKE A PERFORMER. I KIND OF LOOK LIKE I'D BE YOUR MATE'S BROTHER, SO I'M QUITE ACCESSIBLE IN THAT SENSE."

ED SHEERAN

his school year who didn't go to university.) In the main, however, it's about the wrench of parting and knowing that, despite their friends thinking they'd always be together, the relationship was over. He finds her hairband in his room and that sets off a "tsunami" of yearning; he gets high to try to forget but it doesn't work; he gets drunk again, to no avail. He raps some of the verses, racing through them with a fair bit of dexterity, but his flow is defiantly "nice home-counties kid". Yet that's part of his appeal – he knows he's no MC but he couldn't care less if he's uncool, which makes him... well... pretty cool.

GRADE 8

Essentially an amiable shuffle, "Grade 8" is another song inspired by the ex-girlfriend of "U.N.I." This time, it's a happier song; he likens her to a guitarist who's reached the highest grade in UK music exams – 8. She's twanging his heartstrings as if she were a certified Grade 8, and his euphoria explodes all over the song. "I had a wicked girlfriend when I was 17," he told MTV, adding that + "is pretty much about her." It's not hard to tell that the song was spawned by very young love.

The similes are the kind of thing an infatuated 17-year-old would write: her body reminds him of a biro, he promises never to hurt her, he'll keep the relationship secret if she wants him to. Booze rears its head again but this time he's drinking to celebrate, rather than to forget.

Thanks to co-writers Robert Conlon and Sukhdeep Uppall, also known as grime outfit True Tiger, "Grade 8" is driven by clattering hip-hop beats, a stark contrast to his feathery, folky vocal. It's got to be said that, despite his love of hip hop's propulsive force, Sheeran and roughcast beats go together like vegans and McDonald's. But, despite the mismatch (or maybe because of it), there's something satisfyingly off-kilter about "Grade 8".

BELOW: London grime group True Tiger (since disbanded), some of whom co-wrote "Grade 8".

OPPOSITE: At the Lovebox Festival, Victoria Park, London in July 2011.

WAKE ME UP

Radio 4's Kirsty Young sees Sheeran as "a musical storyteller for the modern age," and this unembellished piano ballad provides proof. It's so autumnal that it's hard to believe he wrote it while lolling beside actor Jamie Foxx's pool in Los Angeles. (The still-unsigned Sheeran had decamped to California in 2010 and met Foxx at an open-mic night. They became friends and he stayed several nights at Foxx's house.)

As with nearly every other song on +, there are many deeply personal references to his relationship with girlfriend Alice, to whom he lovingly penned a note in the thank-you section of the album's sleeve notes. The date of their actual break-up is hard to certify because they split several times before finally ending things for good. It would appear that, at the time the song was written, they were very much on but, by the time the album came out, things were less certain.

You wonder how Alice herself felt about his openness but the album offers no hints. We only hear Sheeran's version of events, which mainly portrays her in a highly positive light. "Wake Me Up", for instance, is an opportunity for Sheeran to go swoony about her loveliness – the green eyes that look grey in some lights, the lashes that are long enough to flutter against his skin, her way of tossing her hair back.

"I picked out every little thing [I liked] about my ex-girlfriend and put it in a song," Sheeran told the *Sun*. That included her fondness for *Shrek*, her ability to put away as much drink as he does (and *he's* drunk regularly, he tells her admiringly), her laughter when her brother beats him at video games. But the most affecting moments in the song are when he recounts the little gestures he's made to prove his love. They went to Southwold one New Year's Day, for instance, and he carved two pieces of chalk into a heart for her. He's wondering whether he should get a tattoo of her name, which would be a big decision, because, at that point, he hadn't properly started the tattoo collection that would grow to cover both arms and his chest. In another verse, he looks at his left hand and wishes there was a ring on the fourth finger.

This track is the album's best example of Sheeran's occasional journeys into Snow Patrol-style MOR intimacy. Fittingly, he later covered Snow Patrol's hit "Chasing Cars" and has written numerous songs with guitarist Johnny McDaid, including "Shape of You".

RIGHT: With Jamie Foxx, his LA "landlord", at the Stevie Wonder All-Star Grammy Salute. Los Angeles, February 2015.

OPPOSITE: At a gala for one of his favourite charities, East Anglia's Children's Hospices. Natural History Museum, London in November 2016.

SMALL BUMP

Sheeran had a friend – some say it was a girlfriend but this appears to be incorrect – who miscarried in the fifth month of pregnancy. Her loss spawned one of his most naked songs and one of only three on the standard version of + that was written by him alone.

Told from the mother's point of view, "Small Bump" deftly captures the anticipation and wonderment of pregnancy. Considering that it was written by a teenage boy, the song is remarkably believable; the picture he creates of vulnerability – tiny fingers clutching the mother's thumb – rings true.

The sparse track, comprised of just his voice and guitar, isn't one of his conversational songs; there's none of the stumbling-across-my-girlfriend's-jumper-in-the-laundry-basket familiarity. "It was quite a difficult subject to tackle," he said to *Interview* magazine. "It's quite a touchy subject, so I wrote it

from the perspective of actually being the parent." It would have been easy to give in to cloying sentiment but it avoids that until the last line, when Sheeran muses that life works in mysterious ways and that, perhaps, the baby was needed in Heaven.

He also uses the device of not letting on until the final verse that the baby was stillborn – until then, it seems to be about Sheeran himself, conveying his joy at impending fatherhood. Adding weight to that theory, at the beginning, he apologises to the baby for lumbering him/her with his ginger hair. Only in the very last line is it revealed that the baby has died. That sign-off adds kapow but it wasn't enough to get "Small Bump", the album's fifth single, higher than Number 25 in the UK chart; in Australia, where his releases often outperform his UK placings, it was Number 14.

THIS

Co-written by Gordon Mills Jr, son of Tom Jones'
first manager, "This" is tucked away in the middle of
+. Mills' involvement may or may not explain why
the song lacks Sheeran's usual densely woven lyrical
landscaping. Instead, it's three standard minutes of
amorous misadventure: Sheeran's girl leaves him and
quickly takes up with another man, leaving Sheeran
brooding on the side-lines.

Were it a typical Sheeran song, there would be a
good deal of scene-setting and, perhaps, a disparaging
description of his romantic rival. Here, though, the
lyric is full of woolly yearning: what they had was
beautiful, he threw it all away, now he has to watch
her snuggling with the new boyfriend. Can they get
back together? We're left with the sense that they will.

Despite its pretty, unadorned melody and one of
Sheeran's most heartfelt vocals, "This" is unsatisfying
because of its lack of singularity – it's just as easy to
picture it being sung by James Bay or Harry Styles. There
were plenty of people who couldn't understand the fuss
about Sheeran, and "This" heightened their conviction
that he was just an average Joe who'd got lucky.

THE CITY

Sheeran says he left home at 16, having persuaded his parents that he had to be in London to have any chance of making it in music. He went with the blessings of his father, who encouraged his interest in music, but against the wishes of his mother, who wanted him to go to university.

A paean to his adopted home, "The City" is an impressionistic jumble of tower blocks, 24-hour convenience stores and drug paraphernalia discarded in the gutter. Having recently arrived from Framlingham, this "country boy" is struggling to find his feet – you can picture him wandering around in wide-eyed wonder. The lyric does feel like the product of a teenage writer, especially since Sheeran, who rarely resorts to cliché, willingly falls back on it here. Take the very first line, in which he declares that London is the place that – yes – "never sleeps".

Still, it's a very likeable hymn to the capital. Where others saw squalor, he saw opportunity: the grubby pavements were perfect for busking, the anonymity allowed him to work on his music. The song was written during his first year in London and a rudimentary version came out in 2009, on the self-released EP *You Need Me*. Sheeran liked it enough to include a live version on the 2010 EP *Loose Change*.

The early version was folk-influenced with added beatboxing but, by the time he re-recorded it for +, it was a genre-bending hybrid of R&B, trip hop and pop. Of all the songs on his debut, "The City" most captures Sheeran's musical blurred-lines approach: he was as much an R&B fan as he was a classic troubadour. That was why he caught the ear of teenagers. Like them, he'd grown up with hip hop and was blending it with wildly melodic, folkish choruses. It didn't hurt that he was a sensitive soul and, clearly, a decent sort to boot His EP releases, by the way, were part of the two-

pronged approach he'd adopted by age 13 to get himself noticed. He was starting to gig as often as possible and, from January 2005, also put out a string of EPs that, along with the gigging, created word of mouth about him. It's safe to say that, without the EPs, recognition would have been slower in coming. He burned them onto CDs himself and sold them out of his rucksack in the early years, sometimes relying on sales to make enough money for the train fare home.

Between 2005 and early 2011, when he signed his record deal, there were eight. The last five were repackaged in 2015 as a box set titled 5, which filled the release gap between x and ÷ but also posed the question: why only the last five? The first three were interesting in their own right as both a testament to budding talent and a career-document.

For instance, the extended-play he put out when he was 16, "Want Some" ("some" probably referring to music, rather than fisticuffs), shows significant promise, as well as an indisputably teen world view. Sheeran's voice is pure and choirboy-ish and his guitar work simple but effective. He and his six-string work through a clutch of songs whose titles reveal they were definitely dreamed up by a 16-year-old: "I'm Glad I'm Not You", "You Need to Cut Your Hair", "I Can't Spell".

But the music is much more mature than the titles suggest. At some point during their school years, most adolescents lose their hearts to some bewitching classmate and a few even write poetry about it. What most don't do is turn the experience into dreamy, articulate songs with proper verse-verse-chorus structures. And, at 16, Ed was already acquainted with the pitfalls of romance. "You Need to Cut Your Hair" contains the line "Don't give in to lust" – advice from his father, urging him not to get involved with a local femme fatale.

LEFT: Performing at Camp Bestival, Lulworth Park, Dorset, July 2011.

OVERLEAF: On stage in Hamburg, May 2012.

LEGO HOUSE

The third single from +, "Lego House", was also the third in a row to reach the UK Top 5. Along with the chart-topping performance of +, which came out in September 2011, it confirmed that Sheeran was the biggest new act of that year.

The version of "Lego House" that made it onto the album was a long way from what he originally envisaged. He wrote it as a slow, drum-heavy dubstep track, accented with synths, and "my voice Auto-Tuned to hell, kind of like a T-Pain thing." He kept the original demo on his phone and it sounded weird, he said, compared with the acoustic ballad that it became. It's one of the strongest of his early singles: the chorus surges majestically and his rap in the middle is a neat counterpoint to all the lushness.

Again, the subject was a break-up, with Lego employed as a metaphor for the fragility of relationships: all the painstaking work of putting Lego together can be undone in an instant if it's dropped. Lego had special significance for Sheeran. It was one of his favourite toys, even as an adult, and was the first thing he bought – a Lego *Star Wars* Millennium Falcon, specifically – to celebrate + reaching Number 1. That wasn't the extent of his love for it, though. He admitted on Graham Norton's chat show, "I once went on a date and brought

TOP: With a pack of Lego at Radio 1's London Studios, November 2011.

LEFT: The first thing he bought to celebrate + reaching Number 1: a *Star Wars* Millennium Falcon.

OPPOSITE: His Lego tattoo, Carlsbad, California in February 2013. Also visible is the tattoo of Damien Rice's signature.

"APPARENTLY, I DON'T FIT LEGO'S DEMOGRAPHIC 'CAUSE I'M A LITTLE BIT OLDER."

ED SHEERAN

a Lego set and made the Lego set and then left." It was a *Pirates of the Caribbean* pirate ship, he added in mitigation. Well, of course, who wouldn't take *that* on a date? There's no way of knowing what part Lego played in the failure of the relationship in "Lego House" but the plastic bricks were also referenced in "U.N.I." – and there was an alternative version of the "Lego House" video in which all the characters were made of... well, you know.

The official video, though, was less jokey. Director Emil Nava went off-piste, interpreting the storyline in a completely different way. Harry Potter actor Rupert Grint was cast as a crazed fan who breaks into his house, plays his guitar and drops his Lego helicopter on the floor, breaking it. In the final scene, he uses his physical resemblance to the singer to get past security at the arena where he's playing that night, and walks onstage to frenetic cheers. That's when the real Sheeran arrives at the venue (actually the University of Hertfordshire's auditorium) and Grint is ejected by two guards.

As he's heaved out the stage door, Sheeran glances at him incuriously for an instant – an agonising denouement for a stalker, to finally meet one's hero and be ignored by him.

In real life, Sheeran has had a semi-parallel experience in which he was the fan, though not an unhinged one. One of the perks of being massively successful is that all the artists he worshipped as a teenager have become friends, or at least acquaintances. All except one.

As he told *GQ* magazine in 2017, "Every single hero of mine has got in touch with me bar Damien Rice, who I've never heard from, even though I've name-dropped him in several songs." When he was 11, he met Rice after a gig in Ireland and was delighted when Rice gave him a memento – a piece of paper with the name "Ed" scrawled on it, alongside drawings of a stick figure and an airplane. Sheeran later went on to have the drawings tattooed on his arm.

ABOVE: Shakedown Festival, Brighton, September 2011 – one of his many festival appearances that summer.

OPPOSITE: Cousin Jethro Sheeran, who raps under the name Alonestar, as the Exposure Music Awards, 2011. He was a support act on Ed's 2011 UK tour.

YOU NEED ME, I DON'T NEED YOU

One of the songs in which Rice was namechecked was "You Need Me, I Don't Need You", his second single. He wrote it when he was 15 and it first appeared on his 2009 EP *You Need Me*. That early version sounded remarkably like the finished item, which hit Number 4 in 2011. The nagging chorus was already in place and Sheeran had acquired the breakneck flow that characterises his rapping. After he moved to London, he was put in touch with producer Rupert Christie, who'd worked with Lou Reed, U2 and Coldplay, and they created a more polished take.

At one point, he toyed with the idea of including bars by his rapper cousin Jethro and also experimented with eliminating the rapping entirely. The track that finally made it onto the album was produced by Jake Gosling and Charlie Hugall, producer of Dizzee Rascal and Florence + The Machine. Before Gosling and Hugall got involved, Sheeran didn't like the track and wanted to leave it off the album – at any rate, he certainly didn't think it had Top 5 potential. Hugall was more enthusiastic, deciding that what it needed was a live drummer. The drummer played along to the track

> **" COUNTLESS PEOPLE TOLD ME I SHOULD STOP PLAYING IT, SO FOR IT TO BE MY SECOND SINGLE IS FLIPPIN' WICKED. "**
>
> **ED SHEERAN**

and Hugall chopped up the drum parts. "It sounded sick," Sheeran remembered appreciatively.

It's one of his wordiest compositions and, on the rapped verses, he spits the lyrics at full throttle, cramming in dozens of images. Contrastingly, the sung verses have a jazzy lilt, as if he'd listened to a Chet Baker album before going into the studio.

He considers "You Need Me" a "sad" song but his delivery rages and flails, and even squeezes in an unexpected "fucking". This is Sheeran with a massive axe to grind. In particular, he's peeved by an early manager who advised him to dye his hair and get rid of the loop pedal if he wanted to make it. Sheeran's retort overflows into bubbling outrage and, to underline the importance of the lyrics, the accompanying video is a simple black-and-white clip that features young actor Matthew Morgan dancing to the music.

Sheeran proudly announces that he didn't go to the Brit School (the South London hothousing academy that produced Adele and Amy Winehouse) and tells the manager he didn't need him anyhow because he's got so many followers on MySpace (if there were ever a brand name that dated the song to the 2000s, itwas MySpace).

At that point, he tells us, his big ambition was simply to have his name in lights alongside Damien Rice's. The wonder is that this jittery burst of spleen became one of the best-selling hits from +.

ABOVE: A dress rehearsal for his own Wembley gigs – here he's at the Girlguiding Big Gig at Wembley Arena, October 2011.

OPPOSITE: With his Madame Tussaud's Waxworks (the real Sheeran is on the right), New York, May 2015.

Sheeran's intention with "Kiss Me" was to write "one of those classic wedding songs." Accordingly, this country-cum-pop tune is straightforwardly romantic. It starts with an Americana-inspired guitar figure before dissolving into meltingly pretty balladry, and then crescendos into one of those vast choruses that Sheeran seems able to write in his sleep. As a wedding song, it would be superseded by his soon-to-be-signature-ballad "Thinking Out Loud" but, in the context of +, it's his big romantic statement.

He came up with the song at the request of his godparents, who had been married to other people but became a couple when their respective marriages ended. "My mother had a party where everyone got very drunk and my godparents got on a train back to South London, and my godfather got down on one knee and proposed to my godmother," Sheeran told concert audiences while touring +. He readily agreed when they asked him to play at their wedding but, when he suggested a couple of his own songs he thought were suitable, they weren't keen.

"My love songs tend to be about quite weird shit like *Shrek* and dead birds," he explained. "They said, 'You could write us a song', and I said, 'Okay, challenge accepted'." The result is easily the loveliest track on + and one of the best love songs of his career.

GIVE ME LOVE/THE PARTING GLASS

The final song on the standard edition of + (there are four more on the deluxe edition and two extras on the Japanese Deluxe Edition), "Give Me Love", was the album's sixth and last single.

It came out in November 2012, well over a year after +'s release and seems to have been intended as a promotional device for UK and US dates that autumn. He spent a large chunk of 2012 on the road, crisscrossing America, Europe and Australasia. Endless touring and all it entails – crushingly early starts, visits to radio stations, pressing the flesh with industry executives after gigs – is often hated by musicians but Sheeran's years of gigging had inured him to it and he viewed it as crucial to progressing his career. Saying that, "Give Me Love" is one of +'s highlights.

It was almost the last thing he wrote for the album, "pop[ping] out", as he put it, after he'd started recording. It almost literally popped out – he had the lyrics written in 20 minutes. "Give Me Love" is familiar terrain for Sheeran, touching on two keystone subjects: drinking and regret. He is tipsy and "in a dark corner", missing his ex and debating whether to phone her. If she would just agree to meet, he knows they could salvage the relationship.

The video, with Emil Nava again directing, shows love to be a bloody, visceral process. A female Cupid strolls around a murky, late-night London, firing weapons-grade arrows at pairs of people. Male couples, female couples and mixed-gender couples all instantly fall in love with each other and begin kissing. Sheeran is glimpsed just once, nursing his heartbreak with a cup of tea in a late-night café. Cupid herself comes to a gory end – shot through the neck with one of her own arrows.

Where "Give Me Love" makes its true impact is in the second section of the song. Having begun slowly and huskily, it proceeds conventionally for the first three minutes, building to a cascading chorus that has "American adult contemporary radio" all over it.

Then it turns into a vocodered, percussive chant that's unlike anything else on the record. The chant pulses as Sheeran breaks first into falsetto and then into jagged cries of "Give me love!" It's +'s most compelling performance. For a time, Sheeran used it as the opening song at gigs: "It starts off very quiet and then it gets very loud, and then it kind of works with the crowd," he told a Connecticut radio station.

The album plays out with a Scottish traditional song, "The Parting Glass", slotted in as a hidden track. Sheeran's a-cappella rendition has a purity of tone that reminds us that he was once in his church choir.

RIGHT: Performing "Lego House" at the Brit Awards, February 2012, where he won British Male Solo Artist and British Breakthrough Act.

> " 'GIVE ME LOVE' IS AN IMPORTANT SONG FOR ME. IT'S GOT A MORE FLESHED-OUT SOUND, WHICH I THINK IS WHERE I'M HEADED IN THE FUTURE. "
>
> **ED SHEERAN**

+ BONUS TRACKS – DELUXE EDITION

AUTUMN LEAVES

Not the jazz standard but a Sheeran/Gosling original, the mainly-acoustic "Autumn Leaves" is pensive and ambiguous. Taken at face value, it could be part of his want-her-back canon but it's really "a song about losing someone, and not in a relationship sense," as he told a concert audience.

The words suggest that a loved one has died but, without Sheeran's usual detailed lyrical guideposts, there's no way of knowing. It's one of his least-performed tunes, making its way onto his setlist only a few times, most recently in 2012. It's hard to see why it doesn't get an airing more often. Written when he was 17, and polished during the + recording sessions, it would have held its own as one of the 12 songs on the standard album track-listing.

LITTLE BIRD

This is the "dead bird" song mentioned above under "Kiss Me". It originally appeared on the 2010 EP *Loose Change*, released on his own label, Sheeran Lock (named after his father John's art consultancy), before being repurposed as Track 14 of the + deluxe edition. It's an example of Sheeran's ability to turn everyday melancholy into a deceptively breezy slice of R&B.

LEFT: From a promotional photoshoot, 2011.

BELOW: The pawprint was stuck onto Sheeran's guitar by a young artist who stayed with the Sheeran family for a time.

OVERLEAF: Performing at Capital FM's Summertime Ball, Wembley Stadium, June 2014.

Many fans read more into it than was intended – despite speculation that the "little bird" symbolised a fading relationship, the real story is far more prosaic but also more poignant.

Sheeran had just finished a string of gigs and was exhausted. Heading back to his place, he and his girlfriend found an injured chicken in the road. "She said, 'Let's fix this chicken,'" he told a UStream concert audience. "Me being me, I wanted a cup of tea and a sleep. So I went to bed and made her make me a cup of tea – and, when I woke up, the chicken was dead." He felt so remorseful that he "wrote a song for the chicken – and her."

GOLD RUSH

English songwriter Amy Wadge, the co-composer of "Gold Rush", was introduced by her publisher to a 17-year-old Sheeran in 2008. Their first writing session, at Wadge's home near Pontypridd, produced nine songs in two days, five of which ended up on a 2010 EP titled *Songs I Wrote with Amy*.

In January 2011, just before signing to Asylum, he requested more writing time with Wadge. "Gold Rush" was one of the tracks yielded by that session. Sheeran sees it as "a happy one"; it flirts with reggae and casts a misty eye back at his school days, when his mother was telling him that this music thing would never work out.

SUNBURN

Everyone has experienced the emotions that follow a break-up: the misery, the self-pity and the conviction that nobody can ever take the place of the person who's gone. This is the theme of "Sunburn", bruisingly conveyed. Comprised of nothing but voice and acoustic guitar, it's as fragile as a snowflake.

The story behind it is less dramatic, however. Sheeran had, indeed, split up with his girlfriend, Alice, who's the subject of most of the songs on +, but he was only 16 and the pair had only just started seeing each other. He was about to go to London to pursue his career and thought they would be better off ending things. The next day, they reunited and were together for the next four years. "But in that day that we were kind of split up... Every single girl that I looked at, I was kinda like, 'But you're not her.'" "Sunburn" originally appeared on the 2009 EP *You Need Me*.

ABOVE: At the Queen's Diamond Jubilee Concert, Buckingham Palace, June 2012.

RIGHT: Performing at Capital FM's Summertime Ball, Wembley Stadium, June 2014.

JAPANESE DELUXE EDITION

SOFA

"Sofa" and "Homeless" (below) made their first appearances on the *Loose Change* EP.

Both were written with English singer-songwriter Anna Krantz, whose music publisher set her up as a writing partner for the up-and-coming Sheeran. His pre-fame years of couch-surfing ensured that sofas occupy a special place in his heart but, on this track, the sofa is occupied by two: Ed and Alice. Lyrically, "Sofa" is a sweet picture of domesticity. They fall asleep snuggled up and, the next morning, still wearing a hoodie that smells of last night's beach bonfire, Ed suggests they stay indoors, drinking tea and watching *Friends* on T4. He could, if she wished, whisk her off to Jamaica, Berlin or Tokyo, but the couch is much more appealing. Musically, this isn't a million miles from 1980s-style electropop, until, halfway through, it evolves into 1990s R&B.

HOMELESS

Building his own myth, Sheeran has said that, during the early years, he sometimes resorted to sleeping on tube trains, or next to a heating duct near Buckingham Palace. "I didn't have the best personal hygiene at that point because I didn't get a chance to shower," he said in his 2014 memoir/photographic book, *A Visual Journey*.

It was during a heating-duct night that he wrote "Homeless". Yet he was never truly homeless and says as much in the song, which is more a dreamy, late-night thought stream than a picture of life on the streets.

There was always somewhere for him to sleep, even if it was on a council estate with heroin smokers or on a night bus, where he listened to his iPod and reflected that he was doing all right, even if he never went to university.

This is a semi-rap ditty, half-spoken, half-sung, with a flow reminiscent of that of Craig David. It clatters along amiably and the twist is in the chorus – he's not homeless, he's just home *less* than he wants to be.

CHAPTER TWO

2014 // ALBUM: X

ONE
I'M A MESS
SING
DON'T
NINA
PHOTOGRAPH
BLOODSTREAM
TENERIFE SEA
RUNAWAY
THE MAN
THINKING OUT LOUD
AFIRE LOVE

FOLLOWING A HIGHLY POPULAR DEBUT ALBUM IS A TASK SO LADEN WITH POTENTIAL FAILURE THAT THERE'S A SARDONIC TERM FOR IT: "DIFFICULT SECOND-ALBUM SYNDROME". AS A MUSICIAN WHO FAMOUSLY KEEPS TABS ON HIS SALES FIGURES, SHEERAN WAS UNDOUBTEDLY FRETTING AS THE JUNE 2014 RELEASE DATE FOR *X* DREW NEAR. IF ONLY HE COULD HAVE SEEN THREE YEARS INTO THE FUTURE. IN EARLY 2017, JUST BEFORE HIS THIRD ALBUM APPEARED, HE WOULD BE TELLING *GQ MAGAZINE* THAT HE WANTED ÷ TO SURPASS *X'S* STUPENDOUS SUCCESS: "I DO HAVE NUMERICAL TARGETS. I DID 14 MILLION OF *X* AND I WANT TO DO 20 MILLION OF ÷."

Those 14 million sales put x into the super-seller leagues and also introduced an edgier, more confident Sheeran – one who was willing to step away (though not too far) from the sound that made him famous. The album was originally scheduled for 2012 but was postponed so he could focus on breaking America. A couple of solo jaunts were followed by a 58-date support slot on Taylor Swift's 2013–14 Red tour, which had the outcome he'd hoped for – opening the door to huge success in the US.

The cottage-industry feel of his debut album was replaced by something you might call swagger – the name x, in fact, was his way of saying that everything about his career had become bigger: i.e. "multiplied". Much of that was the result of collaborating with American super-producers Rick Rubin, Pharrell Williams, Jeff Bhasker and Benny Blanco, who had dragged him out of his comfort zone.

"I started out making another acoustic record and it turned into a neo-soul-funk record," he said on Australian TV in April 2014, as he was gearing up for the new album's two-year promotional cycle.

In fact, he had started to tire of the "acoustica" that had been his stock in trade and now – a worldwide star, and friend of premier-leaguers such as Swift and Selena Gomez – he was ready to move away from it. The most streamed album of 2014 (430 million on Spotify), x won a Brit Award for Album of the Year and was nominated for two Grammys.

OPPOSITE: With his Brit Awards trophies for British Male Solo Artist and British Album of the Year in February 2015.

LEFT: Supporting Taylor Swift on her Red tour at MetLife Stadium, New Jersey, July 2013.

ONE

"One" was written in Perth, Australia in 2011, shortly after + came out and its position as *x*'s opening song is symbolic. The idea for it came to Sheeran backstage at a gig in Perth; of the 12 tracks on the standard release of *x* (or up to 18 songs, depending on which of 5 deluxe editions you bought – to put that into perspective, those 18 were whittled down from the 120 songs he originally wrote), it's the only one about Alice, who haunted most of +.

"It's the last song I ever wrote about her," he later told Music News. "It was a closure for that relationship, and that album, and it was the start of the new album and the start of moving on."

The valedictory feel also seeped into the video, a monochrome clip in which Sheeran played the song in an empty, cavernous Wembley Arena. There was a distinct "goodbye to all that" tone to Sheeran's ruminative voice and gentle strumming.

To a sparse Jake Gosling production, Sheeran makes a final attempt to save the romance, telling a sceptical Alice – who's already had a marriage proposal from someone else – that, if she came back, he would never leave again. It was easy to make that promise when he was homesick in Australia but it was an evident untruth, as the nature of his job dictated that he would constantly leave. Still, he's making a last-ditch effort. He's drunk and gets lost on the way home; when he gets there, he wallows by listening to sad songs. Finally, he asks whether they can at least be friends.

This song is saturated in poetic vulnerability, which was the quality that cemented his heartthrob status among millions of teenage girls. Sheeran is the fantasy boyfriend who not only talks about his feelings and actively *wants* to be in a relationship (indeed, the only time he's ever been single was between February and July 2015, while on a Far East tour), he's even happy to stay home and watch rom-coms with his girl.

He appeals to parents and grandparents for much the same reasons. At a time when the term "nice guy" is considered a euphemism for "misogynistic entitlement", he appears to be a genuinely nice guy in the traditional sense. And it certainly doesn't hurt that the choirboy in him resurfaces in "One"'s hushed, pure delivery.

The song is so characteristically Ed that it was released just after the album's official first single, "Sing",

as an "instant grat[ification]" free download. It was a kind of counterpoint to "Sing", which was so different from anything he'd done before that Sheeran was afraid it would put off fans. (In fact, "Sing" was hugely successful, giving him his first UK Number 1 single.)

ABOVE: Jake Gosling, co-producer of *x*, at the 2015 Grammy Awards, where *x* was nominated for Album of the Year.

OPPOSITE: At the V festival, 2014, where he was second on the bill to Justin Timberlake.

I'M A MESS

Words and melodies come so easily to Sheeran that he dreamed up "I'm a Mess" while in the shower (history doesn't record whose). It was one of the last songs written for x and the one that he thinks best sums up the album. Every song on the record, other than future hit "Thinking Out Loud", is what he termed "a demon song" – written to exorcise the clouds that had gathered while he was on his way to becoming the UK's biggest male solo artist. The music business is, he told Reuters, "a very dark place," and there were times when he "was in the darker side of things." "I'm a Mess" was written when he was at a particularly low ebb.

He also wove in references to a new girlfriend but, for once, there was no heartbreak involved – for Sheeran, anyway. This time, he was the one who had "messed up", hurting her and wondering whether he had lied in telling her that he loved her (whatever the case, they stayed together for another seven months after x appeared). He finally decides to rely on "[his] stomach" – i.e. trust his gut instinct – which rather ends the song on a cliff-hanger. What does his stomach say? We don't find out.

"I'm a Mess" is a simple, folky slow-burner, gentled along by guitar, drums and programmed keyboards, which work up to a cathartic chorus. Whether or not it was written with arenas in mind, that's where it belongs, with 20,000 people singing its peaks and troughs. "After that, I was fine," he said to Australia's news.com. "Writing that song sorted everything out."

RIGHT: Attending the Royal Variety Show in London with then-girlfriend Athina Andrelos, 2014.

OPPOSITE: Justin Timberlake, whose albums "Justified" and "FutureSex/LoveSounds" were longtime favourites of Sheeran's.

SING

Sheeran had considerable misgivings about even recording "Sing", let alone releasing it as *x*'s first single. The crafting of what turned out to be his first chart-topper was driven by Pharrell Williams, whom he'd met at the 2013 Grammys ("The A Team" had been nominated for Song of the Year but lost to "We Are Young" by Fun).

Williams presented Sheeran with a backing track he'd made, which ran counter to Sheeran's way of working. He hadn't used a pre-written track before and, at that studio session, he'd already dismissed a dozen tracks Williams played, mainly because Williams had a proclivity for jazzy chords that Sheeran "just didn't get". When he heard "Sing", which was a skeletal beat at that point, he liked it but felt it unworkable for him. Williams urged him to try strumming along on his guitar and Sheeran began to see the point.

Yet, even after he'd recorded it, with Williams on backing vocals (he's the one shouting "Sing!"), he wasn't sure what to do with it. It was a slice of prime blue-eyed funk, not a million miles from Justin Timberlake's "Like I Love You", and entirely unlike anything Sheeran had ever previously recorded. The Timberlake comparison was intentional – as a long-time fan of his albums *Justified* and *FutureSex/LoveSounds*, Sheeran wanted to produce an equally visceral party-starter.

The first single from a long-awaited album is both a statement of intent and a water-testing exercise; apart from contributing to the soundtrack of the 2013 film *The Hobbit: The Desolation of Smaug*, Sheeran had put out no new music in over two years. Thus, he decided that "One" would be a more representative first single: not only was it familiar enough to reassure fans he

was still their boy, it would also be a war-cry aimed at the other singer-songwriters who'd emerged in the interim. Arguably, Sheeran had paved the way for artists such as Jake Bugg and Ben Howard, who now occupied what he thought of as his "slot" – the niche reserved for a pre-eminent male singer-songwriter – and "One" would be the announcement that he'd come to take it back.

He ran the idea past Taylor Swift, who'd become such a close friend that he played her every song he'd written for *x*, including those that didn't make it onto the album. When she opined that "One" would be a safe but dull choice, he was forced to reconsider. Elton John, who owned his management company (but was

"TAYLOR SAID I WAS MAD IF I PUT OUT 'ONE' FIRST AS A SINGLE. WITH 'SING' THEY MIGHT LOVE OR HATE IT, BUT THEY ARE GONNA TALK ABOUT IT."

ED SHEERAN

not, despite popular belief, his manager), also said that as the first taste of *x* he'd be foolish to release anything other than "Sing". It duly appeared in April 2014 – "One" was released as a promo single one month later as a form of insurance.

It's easy to see why it was such a smash. Pharrell had recently entered his imperial phase, when everything he touched sounded gloriously right; Sheeran's soulful singing and acoustic strumming were flawlessly on point. The choppy chorus, including Williams's bellowed "Sing!", was the catchiest thing Sheeran had ever written. It could hardly avoid springing into the Number 1 spot, which it did in the UK and Australia in its first week (it got to a less flashy 13 in America, though it was still his best showing in the Hot 100 up to that point).

It was also illustrative of what life was like for Sheeran at that point. It recounted a night in Las Vegas that began with getting drunk with Psy, of "Gangnam

Style" fame, and spiralled into a "fucked up" (as he told *Q* magazine) encounter with a woman. The song begins at the point where he's trying to persuade her to consummate their acquaintanceship – an experience that "definitely left me tainted," he told *Q*. Though it's rare to find such a carnal Sheeran lyric, he hasn't completely forgotten himself: even while he's boozing, smoking weed and getting to know his new friend, he's also fretting – he's expected back at his hotel but he's too drunk to drive. Let's hope his car doesn't get a ticket.

PREVIOUS: Performing with Elton John during the 22nd Annual Elton John AIDS Foundation Academy Awards Viewing Party, March 2014.

ABOVE: Chatting with Elton at the Viewing Party.

OPPOSITE, TOP: Ben Howard, one of the singer-songwriters who emerged during the gap between the + and *x* albums.

OPPOSITE, RIGHT: Going home with "Psy" after a party at London nightclub Mahiki, following his set at Capital FM's Summertime Ball, June 2013.

> **" YOU'RE MENTAL IF YOU DON'T PUT 'SING' ON THE ALBUM. THAT'S YOUR FIRST SINGLE. "**
> ELTON JOHN

DON'T

When he composed "Don't", Sheeran could have made the lyrics a good deal nastier, he said, but decided not to spill all the details. Despite his forbearance, the song was pretty nasty anyway and became one of the most discussed items on the album. In a 2017 interview with *Clash* magazine, he expressed regret about putting a certain song on *x* and, although he didn't name it, it could have been "Don't": "There was a song on my last record that I really didn't want to put on, and I put it on, and it really upset someone... but it's a song that a lot of people listen to and like because they can relate to it."

It took a jealous swipe at an ex-girlfriend, who went off with another guy while all three were staying at the same hotel. Because the ex and the rival were apparently big-name pop stars themselves, the tabloids and the celebrity magazines suddenly got

much more interested in him than they'd ever been before. Sheeran had, by this point, dated several pop stars, including Ellie Goulding and Selena Gomez, and, by working out who was in which city when, the tabloids concluded that Goulding and Niall Horan from One Direction were the other parties in the triangle. Another piece of alleged "evidence" was that the word "burn" appears in the song, and Goulding had had a hit called – yes – "Burn".

None of the three ever publicly confirmed it but the story (and song) elevated Sheeran's profile, while becoming a permanent part of what showbiz calls "the rumour mill".

He predicted that "Don't" would be "people's break-up song," which presupposed that ordinary couples would relate to a tale of pop A-listers frolicking in a swish hotel. Yet there's a universality in nearly all of

"THE TRUTH OF 'DON'T' IS THE FRUSTRATION AND ANGER OF BEING CHEATED ON. EVERYONE CAN RELATE TO THAT."

ED SHEERAN

Sheeran's work and the crux of the song – that being cheated on hurts – applies to everyone.

That the song was co-written and co-produced by Benny Blanco, whose name appears in the credits of numerous pop smashes (Katy Perry's "California Gurls" and Rihanna's "Diamonds", to name two), shows the sort of sound Sheeran wanted this time around. Specifically, he was after something redolent of the hip-hop jams he grew up on, and what he and Blanco cooked up did capture the loose-limbed funkiness of 1990s scene-changers such as Warren G's "Regulate". For the first time, too, he used a sample of another artist's song – Lucy Pearl's 2000 single "Don't Mess with My Man" – to achieve the requisite chilled R&B feel. Blanco shared production with Rick Rubin, a towering figure who helped create the hip-hop marketplace by founding Def Jam Records and, later, became synonymous with an elemental strand of hard rock. Sheeran was attracted to Blanco's pop nouse and Rubin's grit, and predicted that, between the two, they would come up with something electric.

And they did. Sheeran's own angry, sweary performance, skimming lightly over the beat, was the catharsis he needed – once the song was in the can, he said, he put the whole incident behind him.

Note that the original version was littered with the F-word but it was subsequently stripped out. "I took all of the explicit lyrics out after a taxi driver convinced me to do it for his daughter. That's the truth," he explained. He would have had to, anyway, to get airplay: "Don't" was the album's second single, and his first Top 10 showing in the Billboard Hot 100.

LEFT: With Harry Styles, Ellie Goulding and Rita Ora (behind: Iggy Azalea, eating dinner) at the MTV Video Music Awards, Brooklyn, August 2013.

ABOVE: Collaborator Benny Blanco with the Hal David Starlight Award he won at the Songwriter's Hall of Fame dinner, 2013. Sheeran won the same award in 2017.

NINA

Sheeran typically goes into unsparing detail in lyrics but "Nina" was the first time he'd actually titled a song after a love interest. He met Scottish singer-songwriter Nina Nesbitt when she supported him at a Glasgow gig in 2011 and they saw each other for a year (she played the ex who ditched him by text in the "Drunk" video).

During the course of their relationship, according to the lyrics, they veered between cosy intimacy – ringing each other every day, her wearing his hoodie – and uncommitted nonchalance. While they were dating, Sheeran referred to her in an interview as "an acquaintance" and the song's chorus even advises her to dump him because his job will always take precedence. Yet she clearly made an impact.

Co-written with Snow Patrol guitarist Johnny McDaid in a hotel room when Sheeran was their support act on a 2012 US tour, "Nina" fuses a sleepy beat and jazzy piano motif sampled from Wretch 32's "Welcome to My World". Musically speaking, the tune is an airy bon-bon, slipped into x's track-listing between the weightier "Don't" and "Photograph".

LEFT: Supporting Snow Patrol in America, 2012.

BELOW: Nina Nesbitt, the face of the fashion label Yumi, posing for the brand in April 2013.

PHOTOGRAPH

When he and McDaid came up with "Photograph", Sheeran viewed it as *x*'s one sure-fire hit. Even if "the rest of the album is shit," he told the *Daily Telegraph*, this would be the life raft.

For a while, "Photograph" was even in contention to be *x*'s first single; speaking to Australian station Nova FM in 2013, he predicted it would "be the one that will change my career path." At that point, "Thinking Out Loud" – the song that did change his career path – hadn't been written and "Photograph" was the exactly the kind of sweeping anthem that clamps itself to the upper regions of singles charts like superglue. When it was released as *x*'s fifth single in May 2015, however, it only climbed to Number 15 in the UK, possibly because "Thinking Out Loud" was so ubiquitous that it had sated fans' appetite for big, emotional balladry.

Based on a three-note piano loop McDaid had been working on, "Photograph" was conceived in a hotel room in Kansas City in May 2012. As McDaid tinkered with the loop, Sheeran was on the floor, constructing a Lego X-Wing Fighter for a charity auction. Gradually, he began to sing along and, once he'd engaged, the tune came together almost immediately. He finished it later, in Denver, on what he thought was 6th Street – the song contains a reference, too, to kissing under a lamppost on 6th Street. Accustomed to marking significant events by getting tattooed, he had a street sign with "6th St" inked onto his left arm, only later discovering that he'd actually been on 6th Avenue.

There's a touch of Snow Patrol about "Photograph": it's not unfair to compare it to that band's 2006 blockbuster "Chasing Cars", which Sheeran occasionally covered at shows. Both songs share a long, slow build to a mountainous chorus and provoke heartfelt sing-a-longs when played live. Where "Photograph" has the edge on "Chasing Cars" is in the fine print – the intensely detailed lyrics that distinguish Sheeran songs from others in the big-ballad category. Where the Snow Patrol hit deals in generalities, "Photograph" is full of specifics. It's not just the lamppost moment but the little things Sheeran noticed in the girlfriend who inspired the song (said to be Nesbitt) – her jeans were ripped, she received a necklace for her 16th birthday, she "whispered" during a phone conversation.

Sheeran's observant eye makes him an anomaly among his pop peers: in an age when self-absorption, as symbolised by the selfie, is the order of the day, Sheeran made his name by looking outward. His story lyrics nearly always focus on what's around him, rather than ruminating about his inner life. Although Sheeran's lyrics obviously contain plenty of reflective moments, when his own feelings surge to the surface, he generally focuses on the events and people around him, rather than wallowing in his own thoughts.

The storyline to the video for "Photograph" only loosely followed the lyrics and, except for the last few moments, Sheeran himself doesn't appear in it as the person we know today. It's a common tactic of his to devise videos in which he plays almost no physical part (in the "Sing" clip, for instance, he was represented by a carousing red-haired puppet). Moreover, the video storylines often diverge from the song lyrics and the video for "Photograph" is no exception. It has nothing to do with missing a girlfriend while on tour but, instead, consists of his parents' camcorder footage of his life, from babyhood to today.

It tracks him literally from the cradle, through piano lessons as a smiley, bespectacled toddler, to a multi-instrumental adolescent who passers-by ignore as he bravely busks on the street, to, eventually, the moment he walks onstage to a cheering crowd at a festival. The festival footage also contains a particularly striking moment, shot from among the audience, where he's only visible as a face on a giant screen. If any single moment persuaded his parents that their second son had made it (he has an older brother, Matthew, who's a classical composer), this would have been the one. It's all laced with an immoderate amount of charm.

A second video for the song came out in 2016, tying in with the film *Me Before You*. "Photograph" was on the soundtrack to the drama, which is about a quadriplegic man and his carer. The new video has the song playing over scenes from the film.

In June 2016, Sheeran was sued for $20 million by songwriters Martin Harrington and Tom Leonard, who claimed that "Photograph" was a copy of their song "Amazing", released as a single by *X Factor* winner Matt Cardle in 2012. The lawsuit was settled out of court in April 2017.

OPPOSITE: *Johnny McDaid and Gary Lightbody from Snow Patrol at Radio Station WRFF, Bala Cynwyd, Pennsylvania in April 2012.*

" EVEN IF THE REST OF THE ALBUM IS SHIT, WE CAN SELL IT ON 'PHOTOGRAPH'. "

ED SHEERAN

BLOODSTREAM

Sheeran was at a wedding reception in Ibiza when a friend offered him MDMA, which he'd never tried. The experience wasn't one of unqualified joy. As he later told Spotify, it made him feel loving and warm, but also anxious and strange, and he spent the next day deciding how he felt about it. He concluded that alcohol was more fun, telling Spotify, "So I've only done it once, and I've told my mum and dad about it."

"Bloodstream", originally titled "Lovestream", was the song he got out of it. Co-written by McDaid, Snow Patrol frontman Gary Lightbody and London drum-&-bass outfit Rudimental, it conveys the anxiety and oddness he felt while on the drug, but little of the love and warmth. The song transmits deep unease, heightened by a twitchy vocal and wordless, hummed chorus. The words have Sheeran vocalising the paranoia roused by the MDMA: he asks God's forgiveness for hurting an unnamed lover, then pleads not to be left alone; all the while, he's aware of the chemicals "burning" in his bloodstream. For a chart pop song, it makes for uncomfortable listening.

The first version that he recorded – semi-acoustic and downtempo – was offered as an instant-grat download in the week of *x*'s release. On downloads alone, it reached Number 60, which isn't bad for a promotional single. Where it really gained traction, though, was when it was remixed by Rudimental. Their drum-&-bass undertow ratcheted up the tension, and the "Mmm-mmm-mmm" chorus is cavernous. This version, out as an official single in May 2015, reached Number 2 in the UK chart and, as Sheeran's most club-friendly track to date, might have landed him on playlists he'd never been welcome on before.

BELOW: Performing with Rudimental at the 2015 MTV Europe Music Awards in Milan. Sheeran co-hosted the awards.

OPPOSITE: At the 2013 Grammy Awards, where he performed "The A Team" with Elton John and was nominated for Song of the Year.

TENERIFE SEA

Sheeran went to the Grammy Awards for the first time in 2013, when "The A Team" was nominated for Song of the Year. He didn't much enjoy it, reporting later that it was full of people he didn't know, talking about things he didn't understand. On the up side, it was where he met Pharrell Williams. During the ceremony, meanwhile, he performed "The A Team", with Elton John chipping in on piano and vocals, and that did his career no harm at all. The rest of it, though, left him cold. "I found myself [feeling] competitive, and pissed off that I didn't win, which felt very unhealthy," he said to the *San Francisco Examiner*.

His then-girlfriend was with him and the night turned out to be a bonding moment. Though he was surrounded by musicians he idolised, neither of them wanted to be there and his feelings for her at that moment turned into a song. The title came from the colour of her eyes, which were "seriously blue, like electric blue", and the lyrics contrasted his adoration of her with his distaste for the industry chatter around him. It was a return to gentle, "Lego House"-style balladry, and its sensitivity and lyrical content has seen it adopted by Sheerios as a wedding song, with more than a few saying that they've walked down the aisle to it.

"MOST GINGER-HAIRED PEOPLE I KNOW ARE VERY OUTGOING AND COMEDIC."

ED SHEERAN

RUNAWAY

We're nine songs into x by this point. We've followed Ed through his final farewell to Alice, his ambivalence about a new relationship, his delight when he meets Miss Right, tales of A-list debauchery and cheating, and of finding the "industry" part of the music business highly unappealing. We're coasting towards the end of the standard edition of the album and the time feels right for one of his acutely observed vignettes about someone he met on the road.

For a guy who yearned for fame, Sheeran has written a number of songs about escaping it all (on the ÷ album, he even unequivocally calls fame "hell"). "Runaway" is one such song, though the lead character is a woman he spoke to while on tour, rather than himself. As with "The A Team"'s protagonist, the woman is in an impossible situation, living at home and confronted daily by her father's alcoholism. She plans to run away but hesitates – she loves "Daddy" and, if he could just pull his life together, she would stay. (Unlike the runaway in The Beatles' "She's Leaving Home", this one

still hopes for a resolution.) Though it's tempting to assume that story songs about other people represent a hidden side of Sheeran's personality – on some level, he did want to run from the demands and responsibilities of the limelight – "Runaway" really was inspired by someone else's life.

This is the album's other Pharrell Williams co-write; its clip-clopping beat and compressed (possibly Auto-Tuned?) vocal identify it as a Pharrell product. Yet it also calls to mind Jason Mraz, the American songwriter whose folkish pop is sometimes adorned with rappy trimmings. Either way, it displays Sheeran's remarkable eye for tiny specks of detail.

ABOVE: American singer-songwriter Jason Mraz, who combines folky pop and rap trimmings.

OPPOSITE: Performing "The A Team" with Elton John at the 2013 Grammy Awards.

THE MAN

Sheeran told a concert audience in Germany that "The Man" is the one song he regretted putting on *x* because it was so personal. Few of his songs stint on intimacy but this one – written in stream-of-consciousness style – is almost a diss track, brimming with jealousy and venom. It was a holdover from 2011, written when he was still seeing Alice. Though Sheeran stated that "One" was his last word on the subject of his ex-girlfriend, he evidently wanted to get in a final "oh, and another thing."

"The Man" demands attention for several reasons, one of them being that, on the rapped segments, his flow and phrasing has arguably been affected by listening to Mike "The Streets" Skinner. Even his accent seems to have shifted a little in the direction of Skinner's clipped Brummie delivery. He doesn't sound much like his "ginger white guy" self but his hurt feelings and sexual jealousy are abundantly clear.

The lyrics read like a 3am rant that ends up on Facebook when you've come home drunk and seething at a former flame. Sheeran careens from disgust that the ex has already found someone new (a former public schoolboy, no less) to a bravado moment in the chorus – he doesn't love her or need her anyway – to a spiralling monologue about the demands imposed by a career in music (if he hadn't been a songwriter, he reckons they would have ended up married; *she* has a normal job but *his* job, he'll have you know, is "24/7").

He's drinking and smoking weed to cope, and worries that he'll end up on hard drugs and die at 27, the age that has claimed so many rock stars. After a final wallow in misery, he admits he still loves her and apologises for the bluntness of the past four minutes. The minimal backing track, comprised mostly of drums and keyboard, complements his raging flow.

OPPOSITE: Triumphant at a gig in Hamburg, 2012.

BELOW: Mike Skinner of The Streets, a likely influence on Sheeran's rapping style, performing in Birmingham.

> ❝ I HAD A LOT ON MY BRAIN, SO I JUST PUT IT ALL IN THIS SONG. IT'S A BIT BRUTAL. ❞

ED SHEERAN

THINKING OUT LOUD

Once Sheeran began headlining stadiums, he had a new problem: how does one man and his loop pedal hold the attention of 90,000 people? This man took tips from people who had been doing it for years: "I've watched a Coldplay DVD numerous times and taken little tricks that Chris Martin does with the crowd," he said with endearing honesty.

The song that elevated him to stadium level was "Thinking Out Loud", which, to date, has sold more than 19 million digital copies (note that digital sales include not just paid-for downloads but also the number of times a song has been streamed for free; at the time of writing, 150 streams equalled one sale). There's a long list of statistics: it won two Grammys (Song of the Year and Best Pop Vocal Performance,

2015), helped to fetch him two Brit Awards (Best Male Solo Artist and Album of the Year) and the Ivor Novello Award for Songwriter of the Year. It became his second UK Number 1, spending 54 consecutive weeks in the UK Top 40. In America, it bedded in at Number 2 for 8 weeks, only denied the top spot by Mark Ronson's "Uptown Funk". And, based on "combined sales" – downloads plus streaming figures – it's the UK's sixth-best-selling single of all time.

OPPOSITE: An intense moment at the First Direct Arena, Leeds, 11 October 2014.

BELOW: With Coldplay's Chris Martin, posing onstage at the 2015 Global Citizen Festival against extreme poverty in Central Park, New York.

As previously noted, Sheeran had been counting on "Photograph" to be his ace in the hole if the rest of the album had been, as he put it, "shit". That was before "Thinking Out Loud" existed but now it's hard to imagine Sheeran's career having taken the same dramatic trajectory if "Photograph" had been *x*'s big-ballad moment.

"Thinking Out Loud" had the qualities that instantly connected with listeners: not just a simple, untampered-with guitar/piano arrangement or an earworm of a melody – once heard, it stayed in your head all day – but a lyric that offered a fresh take on an threadbare subject. It was a love song but one that looked 50 years into the future, when the couple in the story were in their seventies and physically frail but still bound by a deep, decades-long, love affair.

It was striking, and unusual for a pop song written at a time when pop music was almost wholly electronic and producer-led. The 23-year-old Sheeran was picturing an idyllic old age for himself and his future wife (she would definitely be a wife, not a "partner" – he is traditional that way): she might no longer be nimble, and he might be balding, but their bond would have mellowed and strengthened. The woman he wrote it for was his new girlfriend, Athina Andrelos, whom he had only known for a short time – he was at a "really happy point" with her when he wrote it, he revealed. Sadly, after a year together, they broke up.

The last song to be written for *x*, in February 2014, it only came about because Amy Wadge, co-writer of the *Songs I Wrote with Amy* EP, was having money trouble and asked Sheeran if he would put one of their old songs on the deluxe version of *x*.

Wadge went to his house in London and, as she waited for Sheeran to get out of the shower, she began to strum his guitar (a gift from One Direction's Harry Styles, whom he'd met when he wrote several songs for the band). She came up with two guitar lines that Sheeran, on emerging from the shower, decided he liked and suggested they use as the basis of a song. Sitting at his kitchen table at 2am, they wrote it in 20 minutes. He recorded it on his phone and, by the end of 2014, it had become his signature hit. "Now she never has to worry about money again," Sheeran later told the *Daily Mirror*, with remarkable understatement.

The video for the track takes the romanticism and runs with it. And "romanticism" is the word. Virtually alone of his pop confreres, he's unashamedly, publicly soppy about his girls. How soppy? Put it this way: he's

ABOVE: At last: after a string of nominations, Sheeran picked up a 2016 Grammy for Song of the Year with "Thinking Out Loud".

OPPOSITE, LEFT: "Thinking Out Loud" co-writer Amy Wadge with Sheeran at the 2016 Grammy Awards.

OPPOSITE, RIGHT: Brittany Cherry, his dance partner in the "Thinking Out Loud" video.

> **" NO ONE'S REALLY CHANNELED VAN MORRISON FOR A LONG TIME. EVERYONE ALWAYS CHANNELS MICHAEL JACKSON, THE BEATLES AND BOB DYLAN. VAN MORRISON IS A KEY FIGURE IN THE MUSIC THAT I MAKE. "**
>
> **ED SHEERAN**

kept tattooists busy for years, marking every career milestone with new ink, but he's restricted the body art to areas that can be concealed by a suit. That's to ensure sure that, when he gets married, none of the tattoos can be seen in his wedding photos. His tattoos form a dense web across his arms and upper body but the skin on hands and neck is virgin.

The simple but effective video for "Thinking Out Loud" was filmed in a ballroom and followed Sheeran twirling through a spot of complicated ballroom dancing with American choreographer Brittany Cherry. He'd never danced before but was determined to do all the moves himself, which meant training for five hours a day in the middle of a tour. Take an instant to think about that: five hours a day during a tour. While he was at it, he deliberately dropped two and a half stone so he'd look trim in the waistcoat and tight trousers he was poured into. The effort paid off – for someone who had never done it before, he was a more than creditable dancer.

AFIRE LOVE

The standard version of *x* finishes with a sombre remembrance of his paternal grandfather, William, who died in December 2013 after a long battle with Alzheimer's. He had been ill for so long that Sheeran's only memory of him when he was well dated back to when Sheeran was six.

"He never really knew who I was," he told *Music News* several months later. "But it didn't really matter, because he'd always pretend he did." Sheeran started to work on the song two weeks before William died and he finished it on the day of his funeral. It's a poignant song that recounts the family's pain as dementia took first William's memory and then his speech, and contrasts it with the love between his grandparents, which survived despite the illness. The chorus affirms that love is stronger than death – a remarkably sensitive observation from a 22-year-old. His grandparents were married for 62 years and Sheeran has said that their long marriage, and that of his parents, were examples he wanted to follow.

Co-authored by Snow Patrol's McDaid and the extravagantly moustachioed Northern Irish songwriter Foy Vance, "Afire Love" is delivered with a misleadingly light backing track. The rippling piano underlay was adapted from – of all things – the *Buffy the Vampire Slayer* soundtrack, and backing vocals are supplied by McDaid's girlfriend, the actress Courteney Cox, and her daughter.

If the lyrics were stripped out, it would be generic adult-contemporary fare. When Sheeran is slated, that's the charge most frequently levelled; that his predilection for soft balladry often sees him moving towards the middle of the road, if not actually onto the centre line. Despite his hip-hop influences, his critics perceive him as, in his own words, "an acoustic balladeer who sings soppy love songs to teenage girls."

He told the *Daily Telegraph*, "[That's] a correct analysis for an outsider who isn't a fan." His self-awareness has probably contributed to his success as a songwriter: he knows what people say, and why they say it, but, rather than deflecting him from his path, it spurs him to "overshare" even further.

Oversharing (being eyebrow-raisingly candid) might be excruciating when the oversharer is a reality star whose life is exhibited on Instagram but, for a

songwriter, it's a major part of the job. Sheeran *could* have written in abstractions, leaving listeners to puzzle out the meanings behind his songs on lyric-annotating sites (the biggest such site, Genius, is full of ponderings from people trying to work out what Artist A was saying on Song B, and every Sheeran song gets an equally good going-over). If he did use more metaphor and symbolism, he might get more marks out of five from reviewers but it would have been harder to warm to him. His bloke-of-the-people relatability could even be said to be his unique selling point.

ABOVE: Northern Irish singer-writer Foy Vance and his incredible moustache. He is signed to Sheeran's Gingerbread Man label.

OPPOSITE: Performing in Dublin in an Ireland shirt in 2014.

DELUXE EDITIONS

Sheeran pushes the boat out here. There are five deluxe *x* packages, as follows: Deluxe Edition Bonus Tracks, Deluxe Physical Edition Bonus Tracks, French Collector Edition, Wembley Edition Bonus Tracks and Wembley Edition Digital Bonus Tracks. There's a good deal of overlap: "All of the Stars", written for the soundtrack of the young-adult rom-com *The Fault in Our Stars*, appears on three editions; "English Rose" turns up on two; and "I See Fire", commissioned for the film *The Hobbit: The Desolation of Smaug*, on three.

Also included are various B-sides ("Everything You Are", B-side of "Don't"), live versions ("I'm a Mess", recorded at Lightship 95 in London) and a Rick Ross remix of "Don't". Some unreleased songs ("Friends", "Even My Dad Does Sometimes") pop up too.

It's a lot to be going on with but it attests to the work rate of a writer who can see a film in the morning, write its theme tune by the afternoon and record much of it by the end of the day (see "I See Fire").

I SEE FIRE

Sheeran landed this job when *Hobbit* director Peter Jackson was advised by his daughter, Katie, that he was the right man to compose the song that would play over *The Desolation of Smaug*'s closing credits. Sheeran had been a Tolkien fan almost since birth – the first book his father read to him was *The Hobbit* – and he set to work with a will. In a single day, in the middle of a world tour, he saw the film, sketched out the song and began to record it. Deciding that the recording would require violin and cello, he learned the violin part himself. That might not sound so impressive until you learn that, until that day, he had barely picked one up. "Managed to learn violin for a day," he tweeted. "Hope you all dig it."

As per Jackson's instructions, Sheeran wrote a folk song: "I See Fire" leans heavily in a Celtic direction and recalls both the Irish band Planxty, a favourite of Sheeran's, and Led Zeppelin in their pensive moments. In its second half, it swells into a mountain-climber of an anthem. Jackson had advised Sheeran to concentrate on the film's closing 10 minutes, which led him to thinking like a dwarf.

"Every single song I've written has come from a personal experience," he told the Press Association. "I'm not a dwarf yet, so writing a song from a dwarf perspective was a different way of approaching things." It wasn't just the first time he'd thought like a dwarf, it was also his initiation into producing songs on his own.

He took to the producer role with gusto, as could be expected of a musician who hungered for the greatest possible involvement in the recording process. Released as a single in November 2013, the song reached Number 13 in the UK and Number 1 in Jackson's stomping ground, New Zealand.

OPPOSITE: With the cast of *The Hobbit* at the Los Angeles premiere of *The Desolation of Smaug* in December 2013.

> "PETER JACKSON SAID, 'WRITE A SONG THAT TAKES THE AUDIENCE BY THE HAND AND LEADS THEM FROM MIDDLE EARTH BACK INTO REALITY.' SO, I TRIED TO DO THAT."
>
> **ED SHEERAN**

ALL OF THE STARS

"I See Fire", Sheeran's first film song, was quickly followed by another: "All of the Stars", which played over the end credits to *The Fault in Our Stars*. The 2014 film was adapted from John Green's blockbuster teen novel of the same name – a wryly funny story of two kids who meet in a support group for young cancer patients. (Green had never heard of Sheeran, claiming that the only band he listened to was the California indie outfit Mountain Goats, but, by the end of the project, he was a fan.)

Sheeran's job was to write something that was both elegiac and hopeful – a particularly big ask, given the plotline, which ends with the death of one of the main characters. Sheeran found himself "wanting to be sad, yet euphoric and lift people a little bit, which I hope [the song] does." He quipped at a live YouTube performance, "I'm not writing about dwarves or dragons this time. It's... a bit more human." The lyrics are written from the perspective of the surviving character, who faces up to the loss of the other with the consoling thought that the stars will lead both of them home. It could be mawkish but it's not.

It's a ballad that, apart from its place in the movie, was obviously meant to be played live, which it occasionally is – the surging second half induces arm-waving and massed singing along. A video was released in May 2014, the same month that the film premiered, and deserves its slot in the Sheeran video canon on the strength of its last few seconds, when Sheeran appears for the first time. He sings the final line of the song and bows his head – a surprisingly effective and moving ending.

ENGLISH ROSE

Written around the time that *x* was being put together, "English Rose" might have been omitted from the album because it already had its complement of gentle, folky tracks in "I'm a Mess" and "Tenerife Sea". Nonetheless, he thought enough of it to have a rose inked onto his left shoulder and to include the track on the two Wembley bonus editions. Its misty, homesick lyrics compare the buzz of touring America with the more meaningful joy of being at home with his girl.

The Tennessee sky, a funky Memphis bar, the crazy things he's seen on the road: none of it compensates for the significant other he misses. A harmonica solo, starting at 1:30, ramps up the melancholy. It would be interesting to know whether Sheeran had heard The Jam's own "English Rose", a track on their 1978 album *All Mod Cons*, which covered similar yearning territory.

EVEN MY DAD DOES SOMETIMES

In January 2011, around the time he signed to Asylum, Sheeran asked Amy Wadge for another writing session. This tune, originally called "Hold On", came out of it, along with "Gold Rush" (see separate entry). Wadge's close friend was terminally ill and she felt moved to write a comforting song that urged her friend to hang on to life but, at the same time, not to fear death. Wadge and Sheeran quote a line from Dylan Thomas's "Do Not Go Gentle into That Good Night" and Sheeran tells the friend that it's fine to cry – even his father cries sometimes. (A line that starkly contrasts with one on "Runaway", which despairs of a distant father who never cries.)

The change of title from "Hold On" might have had something to do with the number of other songs with the same title but, whatever the reason, "Even My Dad Does Sometimes" is inarguably the better name. In a decade that encourages selfishness and self-righteousness, Sheeran is one of the few pop stars to openly acknowledge the importance of family and to refer frequently to them. Breathy and young-sounding here, he's complemented by haunting slide guitar.

SHIRTSLEEVES

In August 2011, prolific Twitter user Sheeran issued a cryptic tweet about wiping someone's eyes with his shirtsleeves, which appeared to go unnoticed until June 2014, when a song of that name was premiered on MTV. Why the music channel shone a spotlight on a track that was tucked away on the deluxe edition of *x* is unclear but it provoked a flurry of tweets from fans, most wondering why they'd never heard of this "Shirtsleeves" song if it had been around for three years. Propelled throughout by a clip from James Brown's oft-sampled "Funky Drummer", it finds Sheeran once again the cheated-on party in a relationship. Despite the infidelity, he can't leave; in fact, he offers the girl his sleeve to dry her eyes and, when her make-up stains his cuff, he views it as visible evidence of both her unfaithfulness and his inability to stop loving her. The track's low-key production dates it to 2011 – heard alongside the rest of *x*, it stands out in its simplicity.

FRIENDS

"Friends" was another "and also featuring" song that didn't make it on to *x* but had its share of B-side appearances. It was an extra track on both the "Sing" and the "Don't" EPs, not to mention a bonus track on the French Collector Edition of the album. Additionally, MTV featured it. The music station interpreted the track as a glimpse of a friends-with-benefits liaison he was hiding from the rest of his circle, and it can be taken that way, given its verses about "friends" sharing a bed.

It's much more likely, though, that it was written from the viewpoint of a friend who wants to be much more than that and wonders why the girl he desires kisses and sleeps (as in "sleeps") with him but won't commit to anything more. He's been friend-zoned, in other words, and, on the subdued acoustic track, he thinks about his options: he can either accept it and cope with the jealousy he'll feel if she forms a romantic relationship with someone else, or he can cut her out of his life entirely, an equally impossible option.

TOUCH AND GO

A Rick Rubin production, "Touch and Go" was kept under wraps until November 2015, when it materialised on both of the Wembley bonus packages. Sheeran had never played it live, so it was, in effect, a completely new song and its appearance a month before Christmas was seen by fans as a holiday gift. Lyrically, it's a meditation about how being a touring musician makes emotional attachments tricky, while the arrangement is the nearest Sheeran came in

2014–15 to capturing the sound of Van Morrison, one of his idols. The choppy guitar and Sheeran's phrasing, abrupt and raw-boned, are a tribute in all but name to Morrison's early-1970s period.

All that's missing for the "Full Van Experience" is a jabbing saxophone riff, which raises the question of how Sheeran would sound if he decided to base an album on the bright, horn-heavy 1960s R&B that was a major passion of Morrison's. Don't rule it out. Sheeran has an actual 15-record plan, which he's halfway through. Five of his self-released EPs, plus the three albums for Asylum, take him up to number eight and he's already starting to map out the remaining seven.

As a musical sponge who geeks out over new discoveries, he's likely to have explored the music that influenced his own influences, so it's not out of the question that one of those future albums could offer Sheeran in classic-R&B mode.

ABOVE: Legendary producer Rick Rubin.

RIGHT: One of Ed Sheeran's main inspirations, Van Morrison, at the Hammersmith Odeon in the 1970s.

TAKE IT BACK

After hearing "Take it Back", American MC The Game declared Sheeran his favourite British rapper, which, Sheeran said modestly, "was nice to hear." This was another track that was premiered on MTV the week *x* came out, despite not being on the track-listing.

Considering its ringing endorsement by The Game, it's a mystery why "Take it Back" didn't make it onto the standard edition (it does appear on the deluxe and Wembley digital). Perhaps it's because the tune is essentially just Sheeran cracking wise about life as a ginger pop star. It's something he does from time to time – there's a funny, expletive-laden video, findable on YouTube, of him improvising a song called "My Gingers" – his version of MC YG's "My Hitta".

It's a rare pop star who's not just small, pale and red-haired but also a verified sex symbol. Part of Sheeran's appeal is that he unfailingly draws attention to his "flaws" before anyone else can, and "Take it Back" is a prime example of that. Along with a little laddish braggadocio about how much money he's earned and the movie star he entertained in his bedroom, he manages to get in some of his wittiest self-takedowns.

He's the singer, he informs us, who'll be keeping his shirt on because nobody wants to see him without it – and he didn't mind winning *GQ* magazine's Worst Dressed Man of 2012 honour because, as he says, someone has to ("Named No.1 worst dressed male in GQ, glad they noticed," he tweeted appreciatively on 2 January 2013). As for letting a stylist loose on him, forget it; this boy isn't going to be winching on tight jeans for any photo shoot.

CHAPTER THREE

2017 // ALBUM: ÷

ERASER

CASTLE ON THE HILL

DIVE

SHAPE OF YOU

PERFECT

GALWAY GIRL

HAPPIER

NEW MAN

HEARTS DON'T BREAK AROUND HERE

WHAT DO I KNOW?

HOW WOULD YOU FEEL (PAEAN)

SUPERMARKET FLOWERS

BARCELONA

BIBIA BE YE YE

NANCY MULLIGAN

SAVE MYSELF

IF HE'S REMEMBERED FOR NOTHING ELSE, SHEERAN WILL AT LEAST BE ABLE TO CLAIM RESPONSIBILITY FOR FORCING THE UK MUSIC INDUSTRY TO CHANGE THE WAY IT COMPILED THE SINGLES CHART. IT WAS IN RESPONSE TO AN UNPRECEDENTED SITUATION: IN THE WEEK ENDING 16 MARCH 2017, ALL 16 SONGS ON ÷ ENTERED THE TOP 20. ONLY THREE HAD BEEN ACTUAL SINGLES – "SHAPE OF YOU", "CASTLE ON THE HILL" AND "GALWAY GIRL"; THE REMAINING 13 TRACKS MADE IT THANKS TO STREAMING. THE RESULTING OUTCRY – EVEN SHEERAN SAID, "I DON'T KNOW IF THERE'S SOME WEIRD THING THAT [WILL] HAVE TO CHANGE NOW WITH STREAMING" – WAS ANSWERED BY HENCEFORTH RESTRICTING ACTS TO ONLY THREE TRACKS ON THE CHART IN ANY ONE WEEK.

All of which drew even more attention to ÷. It came out on 10 March and immediately racked up 672,000 sales in the UK – the highest first week in chart history for any male singer. Much of the fuss was caused by Sheeran having absented himself from the limelight for all of 2016. He had announced in December 2015 that he was taking a gap year and would spend the next 12 months uncontactable by phone or social media: "...if you love me, you will understand me buggering off for a bit," he said on Instagram. "The 3rd album is on its way and is the best thing I have made thus far."

Rather than springing off in new directions, for the most part, ÷ refined the approach he'd taken with + and x.

His predilection for love songs both sparse and lush is indulged; he raps again and he also finds time, as on x, to roast an ex-girlfriend's new boyfriend. There are a couple of ventures into new-for-him tropical house and Irish folk, but he's still a one-man melody factory. As if he'd appointed himself the guardian of hooklines, every tune on ÷ has a strong, memorable chorus.

OPPOSITE: Photographed during an interview in Berlin in January 2017.

ABOVE: The design for Sheeran's third album, painted by Ed with the help of Damien Hirst's "spinner".

As an aside, the reason that so much pop seems homogenous is that producers concoct tracks composed of near-identical chord progressions and beats, then give them to songwriters whose job it is to write melodies, known as toplining. Some tracks are used on more than one song so, if you think Song X is literally identical to Song Y, you could be right.

During his travels, Sheeran deliberately visited countries where he'd be just another redheaded Brit: places like Japan – where, at that point, his sales were lower than anywhere else – Fiji and Iceland. His trip to the last made the *Iceland Review*, a local news-and-politics journal, perhaps because he was the first pop star ever to severely burn his foot after stepping into a hot spring at the top of an active Icelandic volcano. "I've never had the feeling of dying before," he said to Ellen DeGeneres – but there's always a first time and this was his. The boiling water got into his boot and, when his sock was removed, the skin came with it. He had to be rescued by helicopter. It happened on his 25th birthday, which was made even more memorable when he was given a skin graft. "It was disgusting. When they put the skin graft on, the skin has to heal over it," he said on Capital Radio.

The accident happened in February 2016 but only came to light in January 2017, when he started to promote ÷. For the entire 12-month hiatus, he had been virtually incommunicado, thanks to ridding himself of his mobile phone. That was the key to really getting away from it all, he said: don't be reachable by phone. (He admitted to having had a basic Nokia so family could ring.) He bought an iPad in order to receive email and then, in effect, dropped out for a year. The only drawback, he said later, was that he didn't use his loop station for months and when he got back, couldn't remember how it worked. Not just that: he couldn't remember the words to "Don't" when he heard it on the radio. "I spent a day relearning everything."

A fringe benefit was that his absence hyped up expectations for ÷. Pent-up excitement erupted into a frenzy of downloading and streaming as soon as new material appeared in the form of two singles, released simultaneously on 6 January 2017: "Shape of You" and "Castle on the Hill". At that point, he realised that the comeback was looking promising. Just prior to the singles' appearance, he'd spoken of wanting to equal Bruce Springsteen's success – specifically, the way Springsteen melds great commercial popularity and critical approval.

"IT'S AWESOME MEETING FAMOUS PEOPLE. BUT THAT'S NOT LIFE. THAT'S NOT REALITY I WANT TO LIVE IN. ONE DAY THIS WILL END. "

ED SHEERAN

ABOVE: A one-night pop-up store in Warsaw, opened to celebrate the launch of ÷.

OPPOSITE: With Ellen DeGeneres at the 2017 MTV Video Music Awards at The Forum, Inglewood, California on 27 August 2017.

ERASER

The album kicks off with Sheeran rapping about fame taking its toll, not just on him but on family and friends, some of whom don't trouble to hide their jealousy of his success. He's treated as a cash machine, expected to pick up the tab every time he goes out with them and, when he tries to explain that fame is full of pitfalls, he's told to stop moaning, because this is what he wanted, isn't it? This taut piece of music is both a retort to all that and an admission that, often, he needs help to get by.

He'd followed his heart, just as his father urged him to on their journeys down the A14 when he was 12, and he succeeded beyond his wildest dreams, yet turns to "pain erasers" – booze, drugs, women – to get through the rough patches. He was so hedonistic that, in 2015, the *Sun's* Bizarre column awarded him its coveted Caner of the Year trophy. In 2017, having substantially cleaned up his act, he quipped, "I always said with Caner of the Year that it's cool to get it one year, but two years in a row, it's a problem."

"Eraser" took "seconds" to write once Sheeran knuckled down to it. That was in early 2016, when he and Johnny McDaid had got together for a writing session in Sheeran's Suffolk treehouse. (Yes, treehouse. His pad also boasts its own pub, which is only accessible through a tunnel. No, fame hasn't changed him a bit.) Asylum had asked him to produce another "Bloodstream" but Sheeran wasn't biting. He had a guitar riff and McDaid came up with a beat, but he was unsatisfied. At length, he asked McDaid to leave the room for a minute. Almost instantly, lyrics began to come. "Johnny came back half an hour later and we recorded the song," he told Beats 1 presenter Zane Lowe. "It was just basically vomiting on a song." ("Vomiting on a song": his term for getting things off his chest.)

"Eraser" – he already had the title in his head, for no reason other than liking the word – starts with a lilting flamenco guitar riff, which gives no hint of the verbal torrent to come. The riff loops through the song,

along with hints of guitar, bass and drums. His rap begins with a brief recollection of what he'd done to make it big – from singing in the church choir to years of gig-circuit graft – then enumerates the ways that fame hasn't been what he thought it would be. You can imagine him ticking them off on his fingers: he's envied by his friends, he's lost something of his quintessential "Edness" by getting too caught up in the music industry, he gets no sympathy from people who think he's living the dream. He's decided that fame is "hell" and money only begets "evil".

After promising to use his powers for good, there's a plaintive moment halfway through when he expresses the hope that Damien Rice is proud of him. As previously mentioned, Sheeran has met almost everyone he's ever wanted to, from Eric Clapton to Paul McCartney to Peter Jackson, all of whom contacted him first. Yet he's never heard from Rice, his first and greatest musical hero, and it niggles. He told an interviewer that it wasn't as if he expected Rice to become his best friend – he'd be happy with just an email acknowledging Sheeran's longstanding loyalty. In essence, he wanted Rice to see him as a

peer. That would be the cherry on the cake. For a twentysomething, Sheeran has accomplished many things: he was made an MBE in 2017, appeared (briefly) on *Game of Thrones* and has been turned into a character on *The Simpsons*. What he hasn't had is the thing he really wants – contact with the songwriter who made him want to be a songwriter himself.

On 28 February 2017, he appeared on the video channel of SB.TV, the influential black-music-and-more media company, playing a stark acoustic version of "Eraser". It was 10 years to the day since SB.TV had uploaded its first video and seven years to the day since Sheeran had uploaded his own first video to his YouTube channel. That he was celebrating both anniversaries with a special appearance on SB.TV says something about his standing in grime and R&B. As close friend Stormzy put it, Sheeran was a true

OPPOSITE : Damien Rice, Sheeran's idol since he was 11, at the Italian festival Ferrera Sotto le Stele (Ferrara Under the Stars) in 2012.

BELOW: Sheeran's friend and collaborator, grime MC Wiley, in Boston, Lincolnshire, January 2017.

aficionado of the music, the love for it coming naturally to him, rather than being a hipster poser.

Nonetheless, many had expressed amazement and consternation three years earlier when he topped urban station Radio 1Xtra's annual Power List, which names "the most important UK artists on the current black and urban music scene." Sheeran himself didn't comment at the time but later revealed that he'd known nothing about it and was as shocked as anyone else. 1Xtra's explanation: "... disregarding anything else that we may have considered for other artists, there is so much power in what he produces and writes that this alone holds so much power." That's as may be but his friend Wiley was still discomfited enough to tweet, "We influence a man and all of a sudden it turns he has influenced us! Lol." The two had history: Wiley appeared on Sheeran's *No 5 Collaborations Project*, but by 2012, their friendship had cooled because Wiley had wanted Sheeran to appear on one of his own tunes and he declined. "I did a tune for him, he didn't want to do one for me," Wiley told the *Guardian*. "I know Ed doesn't hate me and I don't hate him. When you get to a certain level, you're not allowed to work with people who are not on your level. That's the problem."

The uproar over the list – which also placed white artists Sam Smith and Disclosure in the top four – generated the following reply from 1Xtra's music manager, Austin Daboh: "Every single day of the week, every single hour of the day we support black artists and other races that make black music sounds. I think that anyone who wants to bring race into the discussion is probably a little bit misguided."

OPPOSITE: In animated discussion after a gig in Germany.

ABOVE: He may have passed on his Caner of the Year crown, but Ed still enjoys a post-gig beer. New York, October 2017.

"THERE IS A DIFFERENCE BETWEEN FAME AND SUCCESS. SUCCESS IS PLAYING WEMBLEY STADIUM AND FAME IS NOT BEING ABLE TO GO OUTSIDE."

ED SHEERAN

CASTLE ON THE HILL

As previously mentioned, the first fruits of ÷ were "Castle on the Hill" and "Shape of You", which came out together on 6 January. Releasing them at separate times wasn't an option, as Sheeran worried that either of them on its own would skew the way the album was perceived. The dual release was intended to flag up ÷'s musical diversity, and you can see what he meant: "Castle on the Hill" was a purpose-built arena track that rose to a triumphant climax in the vein of U2's "I Will Follow", while "Shape of You" was a Rihanna-ish club banger. Noting the difference, Radio 2's Chris Evans asked if "Castle" had been written with the Radio 2 playlist in mind, and "Shape" for Radio 1. Sheeran acknowledged, "Everyone said ['Castle' was] a very Radio 2 single and we need something for Radio 1 as well."

"Shape of You" was so different from his usual sound that, while writing it, he didn't even consider it a potential song for his album. Rihanna and Little Mix were more likely to be able to use it, he decided, and planned to give first refusal to Little Mix. Changing his mind as the song developed, he wrote specifically for Rihanna, whose golden period of dance-pop dominance showed no sign of ending. When he finished it, however, he found it impossible to imagine her singing it, or at least singing a particular line about Van Morrison being on a pub jukebox. In the end, he reassessed the tune, decided it was "actually pretty good" and kept it for himself. It became a worldwide smash, topping the singles chart in 35 countries.

If it hadn't been for "Shape of You" dominating the Number 1 spot for months, "Castle" would undoubtedly

PREVIOUS: Onstage at the Barclays Center, Brookyln, New York on 30 September 2017.

BELOW: The Grade I listed Framlingham Castle in Suffolk.

OPPOSITE: Performing in Times Square, New York, for MTV's *TRL (Total Request Live)* slot on 2 October 2017.

have been a long-running chart-topper itself. As it was, it reached Number 2 almost everywhere making Sheeran the first UK chart artist to debut songs at Numbers 1 and 2 in the same week.

"Castle on the Hill" was the result of a surge of homesickness while he was working in America in the middle of 2015. Yearning for Suffolk's leafy lanes and "backfields", he composed this ode to them. It's drenched in nostalgia, with the Suffolk of his adolescence looming large. He reminisces about rolling down hills, escaping the police by cutting through the backfields (an adventure that probably involved some country-life infraction, such as scrumping for apples) and driving down rural roads, listening to Elton John's "Tiny Dancer". (The lyrics claim he was driving at 90mph but that was poetic license. The lanes near his home were too bendy to allow anything near 90, he later revealed.)

In the chorus, he remembers watching the sun go down behind the castle on the hill. The 12th-century

Framlingham Castle is real, and Sheeran has since been invited to play there, but Suffolk is essentially flat, so "hill" is exaggerating things a bit. Towards the end of the song, he returns to the present, catching up with childhood friends: this one is already married for a second time, that one works in a clothes shop, another has two children but doesn't live with their mother, the brother of another died of a drug overdose, and so on. (Of the girl mentioned in the second verse, who gave him his first kiss when he was 15, we hear nothing, sadly.) The lyrics go on to express yearning to see both hometown and friends again. In 2006, *Country Living* magazine had voted "Fram", as locals call it, Britain's most desirable place to live and Sheeran's attachment to it and his friends has never waned. And nobody else had made "a love song for Suffolk", so he might as well do it.

Although Framlingham is a patch of East Anglia known mainly to those who live there, the feeling of pining for a rosy childhood is universal. Sheeran played the song to Stormzy, and was delighted by the reaction. "He said, 'I can really relate to that' – and he's from Croydon."

The tune was the second one he recorded for ÷ ("Shape of You" was the last) and he listened back to it more times than any other song. "It just sounds completely different," he told Radio 1 on the day both tracks came out. The evocative video, shot in Framlingham and its marshy outskirts, features a group of boys recruited from his old high school who play younger versions of the singer and his friends. The role of the adolescent Sheeran went to Hugo Fairbanks Weston, who looks enough like him to occasionally get mistaken for him around town. Weston's contention that Sheeran is the only famous person ever to come from Fram isn't quite true (soul singer Alice Russell and several sopranos, cricketers and academics also hailed from the area) but he's inarguably the most famous living Framlinghamian. When he met Weston, he had one piece of advice: be loyal to the friends you grow up with.

ABOVE LEFT: Radio 2 breakfast show presenter Chris Evans at the BBC Music Awards, 2015.

OPPOSITE: A 24-year-old Elton John, performing on BBC Two's *Sounds for Saturday* series in December 1971.

"I WANTED TO MOVE INTO A STADIUM ZONE WITHOUT MAKING TWELVE 'CASTLE ON THE HILL'S. I WANTED TO MAKE SONGS THAT SOUNDED BIG, BUT WEREN'T NECESSARILY JUST EUPHORIC STADIUM ANTHEMS. "

ED SHEERAN

DIVE

Since mid-2015, Sheeran has been in a relationship with an old friend from home, Cherry Seaborn, who's the subject of all of ÷'s love songs. Going by "Dive"'s naked vulnerability, the song appears to have been conceived early in the romance, as the pair are deciding whether or not they're in it for keeps. In 2017, Sheeran told an interviewer that they were living together and had a pair of cats called Calippo and Dorito – cat ownership being his benchmark for domestic commitment. In "Dive", however, he's worrying about how things are going. Alluding to his habit of throwing himself into relationships, he's already apologising for having done it again. Writing as a besotted suitor, he begs her not to lead him on the way she's apparently done to others in the past; in particular, he doesn't want her to say she cares about him unless she's sure of her feelings.

Written in March 2016 in a rented house in Malibu, this is ÷'s closest approximation to the Muscle Shoals soul/funk sound of the 1960s. Sheeran's voice aches and rasps as never before and singer Jessie Ware's sudden appearance at about 1:30 adds a soulful complement – a new touch for Sheeran, who had never before used a prominent female voice on an album. His management and label were iffy about it, worrying that it was out of place on a Sheeran record, but in the end it stayed. It was just as well because an eight-months-pregnant Ware had driven to Sheeran's house in Suffolk to sing just the one line, plus a few minutes of angelic sighs as backing vocals.

Later on the track, guest guitarist Angelo Mysterioso sizzles through a bluesy solo as if he were Eric Clapton – which he is. The name Mysterioso has been associated with Clapton in one way or another since the late 1960s, when George Harrison, co-writer of the Cream song "Badge", found himself credited on the sleeve as L'Angelo Misterioso. Sheeran, meanwhile, is rumoured to have contributed vocals to Clapton's 2016 song "I Will Be There" under the multi-purpose Mysterioso pseudonym.

"I'VE HAD ERIC CLAPTON COME TO MY HOUSE FOR DINNER. I'VE GONE TO HIS HOUSE FOR DINNER AND HE TELLS ME THAT HE LIKES MY MUSIC."

ED SHEERAN

"Dive" is one of three ÷ tracks to boast the album credit "Recorded at *RMS Queen Mary 2*" (the others are "Happier" and "Nancy Mulligan"). That's the transatlantic ocean liner he's talking about. Because Benny Blanco, who would produce nine of the album's 16 tracks, didn't want to fly, Sheeran met him in New York and they set sail for Southampton on the *QM2*. Requisitioning a storeroom, the two set up a studio for the week-long voyage. Sheeran's only complaint was that the onboard restaurants had a suit-and-tie policy, and they hadn't brought suits. There were no exceptions to the rule, so they never set foot in a *QM2* eaterie.

OPPOSITE LEFT: With girlfriend Cherry Seaborn, on their way to Warner Music's Brit Awards after-party in February 2017.

OPPOSITE RIGHT: Eric Clapton at the Hammersmith Odeon, 1973.

ABOVE: Accepting the Best Lyrics award for "Love Yourself" with Benny Blanco at the iHeartRadio Music Awards, Inglewood, California, 5 March 2017.

SHAPE OF YOU

Sheeran is renowned for keeping on top of the business side of things, checking sales reports, deciding how to ratchet up his presence in low-selling regions and grinding through months of interviews and TV appearances. When he was slogging through the ÷ promo cycle, were his spirits kept buoyant by the knowledge that he had just released the biggest hit single of his life in "Shape of You"? If they weren't, they should have been. A track that started life as a vocal-and-marimba sketch intended for a female artist became, in US trade magazine *Billboard's* words, one of the "most dominant" hits since 1991. It was ubiquitous throughout 2017, spending 14 weeks at the top of the UK singles chart and 12 weeks as Number 1 in the US. At one point, it was outselling the American Number 2, Migos's "Bad and Boujee", by two to one.

A video interview with American photographer Norman Jean Roy, who shot Sheeran for the cover of British *GQ's* March 2017 issue, showed video footage of him on a London street, gamely modelling a coat in a rainstorm. It would be interesting to know what he was thinking as a stylist fussed around him, but he probably viewed the whole experience as one of the things a guy's gotta do to be enormously successful (though he did later reveal to *Entertainment Tonight Canada*, "I think I look a bit gimpy on the cover"). And what he wanted was to sell 20 million copies of ÷, so getting wet to the skin while wearing a Dsquared2 tuxedo – his normal daywear was still hoodies and jeans – was him simply doing what he had to do.

Fair enough, but when slogging through an album cycle, it helps to be backed up by songs of the calibre of "Shape of You". Funnily enough, Sheeran doesn't especially rate the song, telling Nova FM radio that it wasn't even among his top-five favourite ÷ songs. Nonetheless, he conceded that it was "a really good song to start an album campaign with."

As any savvy businessperson does, he keeps an eye on the competition. While making ÷, he was aware that several other major artists were working on new albums that, if they came out around the same time as his, would siphon away some of the attention ÷ could expect to receive. In the end, he told the BBC he didn't have to worry: "Everyone I was scared of releasing albums around me released them all last year – people

like Beyoncé and The Weeknd and Bruno Mars." His mate Taylor Swift, whose LPs are treated as full-scale cultural events, had scheduled her own new record for late 2017, leaving Sheeran with a clear run at dominating the charts for months. "So I've got a full year of just all Ed, all the time."

Having said that, March 2017 wasn't the original release date. He had planned to get it out in the first week of November 2016 but reconsidered when he realised that it would coincide with a certain American election. That was deterrent enough but, if he'd stuck with November, he would have come up against Bruno Mars' new album the following week and The Weeknd's the week after that.

Aware that all the strategizing made him sound a little too savvy, he told another interviewer that every A-lister is as success conscious as he is. In the hip-hop world, self-belief is the order of the day, with rappers often proclaiming themselves the greatest of all time, so why should he be slated for his own ambition? Every top-flight pop star – not just rappers – is driven

OPPOSITE: Performing "Castle on the Hill" at the Brit Awards in February 2017.

ABOVE: The March 2017 *GQ* cover, itself displayed on a street in Walthamstow, East London.

by a need to be at the pinnacle of their profession, and the fact that he also writes songs for other artists gives him even more reason to be interested in the financials.

When a song is recorded by someone else, the songwriter hopes it will do him/her proud in the sales department. It can be highly lucrative because such songs can be turned out very quickly – the writing session that yielded "Shape of You" also saw three others written that day, all intended for different artists. Because Sheeran didn't feel a personal attachment to "Shape of You", it was never in the running to be on the album and, if it had gone to Little Mix or Rihanna, he wouldn't have regretted it. One negative review of ÷ claimed Rihanna would have turned up her nose at it, which underestimates

Rihanna's gift for recognizing a massive hit, even in raw form.

What's more interesting is Sheeran himself not realizing he'd just penned the song that would propel him to the next career level. Every A-lister can point to a particular song that changed their stature: for Beyoncé it was "Crazy in Love", for Bruno Mars it was his collaboration with Mark Ronson on "Uptown Funk" (which kept "Thinking Out Loud" stalled at Number 2 for eight weeks in the US), for The Weeknd it was the

In the end, the song made it onto ÷ only because Asylum Records pointed out that it would be mad to omit it. The rest of ÷ was already finished when Sheeran, Johnny McDaid and the highly experienced professional writer Steve Mac assembled for the above-mentioned session that yielded four tracks in a day. "Shape of You" took just two hours to fall into place, after which he put it to the back of his mind, not even playing it for the record company. Eventually, he remembered it and had the idea of giving it to Rudimental for a remix. "And [the label] said, 'Why haven't you played us this before?'" he told Radio 1. It was added to the final track-listing just two weeks before the finished album was sent to Asylum.

Why indeed? Part of the answer is that Sheeran is abundantly able to write catchy, radio-friendly songs, and this was just another. The same thing happened with "How Would You Feel (Paean)", which he scribbled as a gift to his girlfriend and promptly forgot about until she said it would sound perfect on ÷, whereupon he gave it a quick wash and brush and slotted it into the album.

As a composition, "Shape of You" is a standard-Ed verse-verse-chorus-verse-bridge-chorus arrangement but it developed wings once a tropical house rhythm, heralded by that bouncing marimba, was added. There's also a distinctly saucy (for him) carnality to the lyrics. Sheeran rarely writes explicitly about sex but here he more or less does. Originally titled "In Love With Your Body", it's about going out drinking with friends and being in the mood for a spot of "sexy time" with someone new. Conveniently, he's soon approached by a girl, who makes it clear that she wants the evening to end in his bedroom. But he wants to chat first, while she wants him to cut the talking and get jiggy. That's the kind of thing that happens when you're a household name.

But there are also some very familiar touches to the lyrics – it's safe to say, for instance, that only a Sheeran tune would contain a line about listening to Van Morrison on the jukebox. On top of that is the opening verse, which is as Ed as you can get. It declares that when he wants to meet someone new for a spicy night, he doesn't search for her at "the club" – no, he prefers pubs to "the club". It's a mythical place, always known in pop songs simply as the club, as if there were only one and they all go there. Sheeran even contributed to a "club" song himself, when he co-wrote "Strip That Down" for former One Directioner Liam Payne.

2015 barnstormer "Can't Feel My Face". Sheeran had already experienced it with "Thinking Out Loud" but "Shape of You" eclipsed it, and more. Its appearance on 6 January took advantage of the quietest time of the year for releases – if you want your record to be noticed, early January is the time to put it out. "Shape of You" would have made a splash whenever it emerged but Sheeran was taking "a full year of just all Ed" literally and launching the campaign as early in 2017 as possible.

> **" 'SHAPE OF YOU' WAS THE ONLY SONG THAT I WAS LIKE 'THIS ISN'T ME AT ALL'. IT TOOK A MONTH OR TWO TO CONVINCE ME THAT IT SHOULD EVEN BE ON THE ALBUM."**
>
> **ED SHEERAN**

But when it comes to his own nights out, he's a confirmed pub/bar man, not least because it's quiet enough to have a conversation in a bar – so it's in a bar that the action in "Shape of You" occurs. In consummate Ed style, he falls for his new friend emotionally. A night of unbridled passion is followed by a date a week later, when he takes her to a cheap Chinese buffet. She seems to like it and they spend hours there, with the song concluding the next morning as he dreamily remembers what happened after they got home from the restaurant. Romantic that he is, he's already a little in love.

As for the actual music, this track cleaves so closely to the house/EDM style that has dominated pop for a decade that it could easily be a Liam Payne (or Little Mix or Rihanna) single. Tropical house is a long way from Sheeran's usual balladry-and-rap territory. Maybe it's Steve Mac's input or, perhaps – as MTV's Anne Donahue put it – what had made him unique before his year-long break was no longer so unique, so he was trying other styles. His "sappy nice-guy love songs" had given him his own slot in 2011, but when he returned in 2017, it was to a music scene full of guys who were also confessing to insecurity and fear of failure. And these weren't just the singer-songwriters who had followed in his wake, such as Ben Howard and Charlie Puth, but the top tier of pop stars, including Drake and Justin Bieber.

There's no way of knowing for sure, and Sheeran hasn't said, but putting out a dance track as ÷'s opening salvo might just have been an experiment to see whether fans would accept him as a dance-pop artist.

Acutely aware that many saw him as pop's sappy love-balladeer, he told Radio.com, "I don't want to be just a one-trick pony and just do acoustic songwriter ballads." Well, "Shape of You" was about as far from that as he could get.

It was such masterful popcraft that it spent 14 weeks at the top of the UK chart and 12 at Number 1 in the US; in Australia, it stayed at the top for 15 weeks. It's one of only a handful of songs to have been streamed 1 billion times on Spotify and its video, showing Sheeran training for a match with (and being thoroughly trounced by) a sumo wrestler, has had well over 2 billion views. The video, by the way, also marked a milestone. The x track "Take it Back" had defined him as the guy who was too pale to remove his shirt in public. For "Shape of You", he changed his mind, or had it changed for him by director Jason Koenig. As he gets ready to fight the sumo champ, who's played by retired Japanese star Yama, he's bare-chested in the training scenes. He wasn't delighted about it but did think the dark, clubby lighting gave it a certain edge.

In March, two months after "Shape of You" came out, the songwriting credits were changed to include Kandi Burruss, Tameka Cottle and Kevin Briggs, writers of the TLC hit "No Scrubs", after it was suggested that elements of "Shape" sounded like the TLC song.

OPPOSITE: Kandi Burruss and Tameka "Tiny" Cottie, who were awarded co-writing credits on "Shape of You".

OVERLEAF: Sheeran and Stormzy onstage at the Brit Awards at the O2 Arena, London, 22 February 2017.

PERFECT

"I think that there was always a scare that 'Thinking Out Loud' would define me and my career, so I wrote a lot of songs, trying to beat it, and I think I have beaten it," Sheeran told Music Choice.

"Perfect", the first song completed for ÷, was the one he meant. In his view, it would not only give "Thinking Out Loud" a run for its money as a tender love song, but, more importantly for Sheeran, it would keep him from being identified with only one song. His worry had been that, decades from now, the name "Ed Sheeran" would be associated with "Thinking Out Loud" and nothing else. His aim was to emulate Van Morrison – you don't have to be an obsessive Van fan to be able to name half a dozen of his songs and, for an extremely ambitious writer like Sheeran, nothing less would do.

With "Perfect", he assigned himself the task of writing the love ballad that would knock all of his others out of contention. No pressure then. Having said that, Sheeran has identified pressure as one of his main motivators, putting him among a small group of artists who thrive on stress. With musicians, stress can either induce writer's block or a ground swell of productivity, and he's one of the latter. When under the cosh, he comes up with the goods. And, lyrically, "Perfect" is the most extravagantly emotional love song he's ever written, with the possible exception of track 11 on the album: "How Would You Feel (Paean)". That one was intended as a private gift for Cherry that would never see the light of day, so he went to town on it with his declarations of love everlasting (brave of him – they weren't even officially a couple at that point). "Perfect", though, was penned for public consumption, so it's a smidgen more self-conscious.

Putting together his third album entailed, as all his albums have, writing hundreds of songs, most of which were either filed away for another time or discarded altogether. After playing a first draft of the album to Rick Rubin and receiving the terse advice to "write more songs," he dropped six songs completely. Whether they'll be repurposed in the future, stay buried or emerge on an Ed Sheeran Rarities collection in 25 years remains to be seen. His manager, Stuart Camp, laughingly told *Music Business Worldwide*, "Ed always comes back with his old songs and we turn him round and say no. Again."

When ÷ was still at the concept stage, Sheeran already knew what he wanted. There had to be a hip-hop track, a big anthem or two, at least one folk song and a wedding song. Of the hundred-odd tunes written, there was "a bunch of wedding songs, I guess," he told the BBC, of which "Perfect" best filled the bill. In Sheeran's opinion, it was indisputably better than his other big wedding number, "Thinking Out Loud". As he worked on "Perfect", he kept in mind an image of couples walking down the aisle to it, and went for the same lavish romanticism that defined "Thinking Out Loud" - albeit with a slight nod in the direction of his Irish paternal grandparents. There's a just-perceptible Celtic lilt in his voice during the first minute of the track; the vocal floats atop a sustained Hammond organ note that adds a churchy feel, and a 21-piece string section sweeps in and transports the song to a day-dreamy cloud.

Lush as it is, it manages to be surprisingly tasteful. Although Sheeran has been described – mainly by American rock critics – as "emo" (emotional), one thing he doesn't do is over-emote. Given enough of a grudge, he might issue a tense rap or, when unsure of his love prospects, he might rasp and claw, as on "Dive" but on blissed-out love declarations like this, he often downplays his vocals and lets the lyrics do the talking. the *Guardian's* Harriet Gibsone thought differently; in her view, "Perfect's" "ostentatious Disney strings and lyrics [were] drenched in supine sentimentality [that] recalls Westlife's 'Flying Without Wings'."

While "Thinking Out Loud" was a love ballad that focused on the distant future, "Perfect" is one anchored in the now, and far more impassioned. Sheeran professes his adoration for Cherry and that he wants them to have children together. The reference to children provided no end of fuel for showbiz writers, who took it as an announcement that Sheeran was ready for them and wanted Cherry to begin producing them. Sheeran bemusedly told interviewers that being ready(ish) to be a father was some way removed from imminently being one.

OPPOSITE: A selfie with James Blunt and fans on the red carpet at the ARIA Awards, Sydney, 26 November 2015.

She looks "perfect tonight", the song goes on to say – a possibly intentional nod to Angelo Mysterioso's 1977 hit "Wonderful Tonight". The chorus reminisces about the night he and Cherry danced barefoot on the lawn to their favourite song, which actually happened, though the lyrics don't reveal that it was at James Blunt's place in Ibiza (Blunt and Sheeran were close friends, having written songs and toured America together, with Blunt as support act). Also unsaid is that the song was "March Madness" by American rapper Future – "the least romantic song in the world," Sheeran admitted to *Entertainment Tonight Canada*. Maybe it's not the least romantic but it has to be in the running. It features the highly acclaimed Future graphically explaining that when it comes to spreading the love, he's equal-opportunities. He's willing to share his bed with "cougars", "basic" girls, even "average" girls. Conscious of having a reputation to maintain, he adds that it wouldn't have happened with the average one if he hadn't been on Ecstasy. A man has standards, eh?

"Perfect" wasn't just the first song completed for ÷, it was also one of only two written by Sheeran alone. This was deliberate. On "Thinking Out Loud", the songwriting royalties were split with Amy Wadge and he'd decided that if he wrote another big ballad, he wanted his name alone on the credits. To that end, he composed many songs solo but only one other, "How Would You Feel (Paean)", made it onto the record. The other 10 LP tracks (or 14 on the deluxe edition) were co-credited to major writing talent such as Benny Blanco, Julia Michaels and Ryan Tedder.

The latter is best known as a songwriter/producer for others but has a parallel career as frontman of the band OneRepublic, so he's a kindred spirit who understands

Sheeran's dual life as singer and writer-for-hire. He and Sheeran wrote more than 20 prospective ÷ songs together, though only "Happier" reached the album. When Tedder told the BBC that Sheeran was "savvier than just about anyone I've ever met" – and he's met Beyoncé and Adele – he was really saying something. Sheeran, he remarked, is "just laser-focused". Sheeran returned the favour by calling Tedder "a really cool hang" – American speak for "fun to be with".

OPPOSITE LEFT: American MC Future at the Summerfest Music Festival Milwaukee, Wisconsin, 8 July 2017.

ABOVE: Performing on the TV talk show *Che Tempo Che Fa* in Milan, 12 March 2017.

OVERLEAF: On the Pyramid stage on 25 June 2017 at the Glastonbury Festival – the first time he had headlined the iconic event.

GALWAY GIRL

If a Sheeran song can be said to be controversial, it's this one. Ostensibly, an agreeable half-rapped folk ditty about a smoochy encounter with an Irish woman he met outside a bar on "Grafton Street", it provoked a wave of criticism in the music media. Some of the sniping was due to a simple inaccuracy – the song led listeners to assume that Grafton Street is in Galway when it's actually in Dublin (to be fair, it doesn't specifically claim that Sheeran met his Galway girl in Galway). Not only that, there are no bars in Dublin's Grafton Street anyway. One Irish website even tried to work out exactly where in Grafton Street they might have met, concluding that it could have been a pub in a side street.

But that was minor carping compared to what really riled the critics. First, they complained that the song evoked memories of The Corrs, whose polished-up version of traditional Irish music made them hugely popular in the late 1990s but was also held to be impossibly tame. Second, the lyrics to "Galway Girl" were full of Gaelic tropes, such as Guinness, "Carrickfergus" and Jameson, which were considered culturally lame. Third, adding even more fuel, Van Morrison turns up in the lyrics again. Not only that, he's back on "the jukebox". While the Morrison reference in "Shape of You" added a dash of quirkiness to a tropical-house track, in the context of "Galway Girl", it was perceived as just one more Gaelic cliché.

And, of course, the song subjected Galway women themselves to the same broad-brush portrayal. This particular girl got roaringly drunk, stood on a stool to sing "Carrickfergus" at the top of her voice and beat Sheeran at darts and pool. The lyrics declared that she was even the fiddle player in a traditional Irish group. That last detail induced scorn in many, who thought it all too convenient that Sheeran's supposed Galway

fling was with a woman who happened to be a trad fiddler. Then, in true Ed fashion, the song culminates in her taking him back to her place, where they drink wine and finish off a bag of Doritos, rousing yet more scorn – why Doritos, many fumed, instead of the proper Irish snack, Taytos?

The woman genuinely existed, however, and really did play fiddle. But that didn't matter – Sheeran's depiction of her was still deemed a lazy cultural stereotype; *Pitchfork's* reviewer, Laura Snapes, cuttingly wondered whether he would portray a French girl with a string of onions around her neck, or an Austrian in a dirndl skirt.

The music site Noisey rounded up some real-life Galway girls to ask whether they felt insulted. Were they, for instance, offended by the line about the Gaelic tattoo on his arm? In the song, the Galway girl asks

him what it means and Sheeran translates. Were they irritated, wondered Noisey, that an English man is seen to be teaching an Irish woman her own language? Disappointingly for Noisey, few of the women were bothered and several were even pleased that Galway's girls were being celebrated by one of the world's most famous singers.

And the Galway Girl of the title? She loved it. Niamh Dunne, fiddler in the traditional group Beoga, told RTE Entertainment, "I'm so happy with 'Galway Girl'.

OPPOSITE: Niamh Dunne, the"inspiration" for "Galway Girl", performing with Beoga at the 2017 Cambridge Folk Festival.

ABOVE: The Corrs at the Kew the Music summer festival at Kew Gardens, London, July 2016.

> ❝ 'GALWAY GIRL''S PROPER MARMITE, WHICH IS GOOD. I GET CALLED 'BEIGE' A LOT BUT I CAN'T BE BEIGE IF IT'S SPLITTING THIS MUCH FUCKING OPINION. ❞
>
> **ED SHEERAN**

Ed Sheeran knows how to write a great pop song and it's so catchy."

Two additional points: Dunne is actually from Limerick, and she's married. She met Sheeran through her husband, Sean Og Graham, who's Beoga's accordionist. (The full five-piece Beoga line-up can be heard on "Galway Girl" and album tracks "Happier" and "Nancy Mulligan".) There was no fling, no wolfed-down Doritos and she didn't even beat him at darts. What did happen is that meeting her implanted the kernel of a song idea and he made up the rest of the story. It wasn't even going to have "Galway" in the title. There was already a song called "Galway Girl" by American country rocker Steve Earle, so Sheeran experimented with other names – Clonakilty Girl, Cork Girl, even Belfast Girl – before deciding none of them had the same alliterative punch.

Talking to *Entertainment Weekly*, he marvelled at how polarising the tune was. It was the first thing he'd ever done that had rubbed so many people the wrong way – not only did they hate it but they were "offend[ed] that the song exists." Looking on the sunny side, though, he reckoned that at least it exonerated him from the oft-levelled accusation that he was bland. If he were that bland, he maintained, "Galway Girl" wouldn't be so divisive. The haters must have enjoyed the video – 3 minutes and 19 seconds of Sheeran having an

uproarious night out in Galway, which ends with him being decisively punched to the floor by a local.

Ed admitted that he'd had to talk his label into letting him put it on the album. They were openly unenthusiastic, taking the view that a folk song – particularly the sort played on tin whistle and bodhran – would be unsaleable to his audience. (Benny Blanco, for his part, thought it was the worst thing Sheeran had ever done.) Sheeran argued that The Corrs' 20 million record sales proved there was an appetite for it; the label riposted that that had been 20 years ago. Sheeran finally got his way by pointing out, as he told the *Guardian*, that there are "400 million people in the world who say they're Irish, even if they're not Irish. You meet them in America all the time: 'I'm a quarter Irish, and I'm from Donegal.' And those type of people are going to fucking love it."

Which they do. As well as reaching Number 1 in Ireland and Number 2 in the UK, it's a major concert favourite. The audience reaction to both "Galway Girl" and "Nancy Mulligan" can be stupendous, as noted by critic Harry Harris in a review of a Glasgow show for the *Daily Telegraph*: "When you've seen thousands of screaming Glaswegians trying to river-dance to them, they make more sense."

RIGHT: *Performing at Croke Park, Dublin, 24 July 2015.*

HAPPIER

Another song conceived on the *Queen Mary 2* and produced by Benny Blanco, "Happier" is a piece of classic Sheeran balladry. It starts small, with just voice and guitar and a line that informs us that he's at the corner of 29th Street and Park Avenue in Manhattan. Slowly, it builds a head of steam. He's joined first by a string section – that's him playing cello, by the way – and then by a backing choir that includes Jessie Ware and Beoga. A full-blooded chorus is followed by a wordless, many-voiced chant and he plunges into the chorus again, cymbals crashing and all hands on deck. It plays out with Sheeran alone once more, whisper-singing the chorus.

He's back to the subject of heartache and there's nobody in pop whose heart aches like Sheeran's – at least, nobody who describes it so realistically. The twist in this particular story, which was triggered by seeing old girlfriend Alice with her new guy, is that he's now detached enough to acknowledge that she looks much happier than she did when they were together. He even admits that the new boyfriend is more deserving of her love than he was. He told the Just Jared Jr website, "[I met] him one day and [realised] 'He's so more suited to her than I ever was' and seeing them together... we were never that sort of couple, never that happy."

And so, while he was bitter when Alice left, it's now been a month and he's processed his feelings. He can watch the new couple walk down the street together without undue misery. Seeing an ex-partner with someone else is often the worst thing about a break-up but Sheeran has reached the point where he's OK with it. As he told Spotify, "It's very much like, 'I'm really happy that you're happy and with someone that you love, and they are really happy that I'm happy and with someone.'" It was a song about maturity, he added.

It was, yet it wasn't. Despite the bravado, the tune is steeped in melancholy. He remembers how much he'd loved her, and is drinking to block it out. His friends are telling him to be patient – the right girl will come along – but the take-away message is: if things don't

LEFT: A selfie with fans at the *C'Cauet* show's Emission Speciale in Paris, 28 February 2017.

" I DIDN'T REALLY LIKE 'HAPPIER' AND THEN BENNY TOOK THE DRUMS OFF IT. THEN, I WAS LIKE 'AH, OH, ACTUALLY, THIS HAS SOMETHING'. "

ED SHEERAN

work out with the new guy, Ed will be waiting for her. In real life, however, things were decidedly different. When he wrote "Happier", he'd long since moved on from Alice and was committed to Cherry Seaborn. Six years had passed since the split and he was now wholeheartedly pleased that Alice was with someone who gave her what he couldn't.

So why did "Happier" give the impression that he and Alice had only just parted? Artistic licence, apparently. Everything described in the lyrics had happened; he really had seen the new couple together and desperately wished himself back with Alice. And, thereafter, he genuinely did reach a point where he could be unselfishly happy for her. But the real story had evolved over a four-year period, rather than taking place in one distraught moment on a street corner in Manhattan. To amplify the drama, Sheeran had compressed the whole thing into 3 minutes and 27

seconds of ravaged feelings, explaining to the Dutch network RTL that that had made it "a bit more 'song'."

In a stinging review in *Pitchfork*, Laura Snapes called his continued interest in Alice "barely suppressed creepiness", which feels unfair. His behaviour seems not creepy but the kind of wistful gazing back that occasionally leads everyone to look up old boyfriends/ girlfriends on Facebook just to see how they look now. He might still be mining long-gone relationships for subject matter but it's no more than every songwriter does, not least critical favourite Taylor Swift.

OPPOSITE: With "cool hang" Ryan Tedder of OneRepublic at the 58th Grammy Awards in Los Angeles.

ABOVE: Jessie Ware performs at the T in the Park Festival at Strathallan Castle, Scotland in July 2015.

NEW MAN

Sheeran intended this indie-rap number, delivered in a crotchety whine that crossed Mike Skinner and "Sheila" hitmaker Jamie T, to be a bonus track but Asylum insisted it go onto the standard edition, where it would get more attention. It's no surprise that he argued against it. Though it follows "Happier" in the track sequence and, on first hearing, seems to take up where "Happier" left off, "New Man" is actually ÷'s comic-relief moment.

Sheeran and Jessie Ware had booked a writing meeting to compose songs for her and, after they'd come up with a couple, she suggested they do one for him. Funny she should say that; he happened to have an idea right there. For a while, he had wanted to write what he called "a fuckboy anthem" and that was the genesis of "New Man", which came out sounding like a companion piece to the previous album's aggrieved "Don't".

The definitive explanation of "fuckboy" comes from Killer Mike, the Atlanta-born MC of the hip-hop duo Run the Jewels: "They are always doing … just the dumbest, weirdest, lamest possible shit." Sheeran, however, has used it to denote a man who's an emotionally manipulative, responsibility-shirking player, which comes under the same umbrella.

The "new man" thus portrayed wasn't someone Sheeran knew – not even his ex's new boyfriend, though many listeners assumed it was him. It's essentially a parody based on a stereotype. Sheeran

BELOW: Jessie Ware, co-writer of "New Man", performing at the V festival, 2015.

OPPOSITE: A typically impassioned Run the Jewels set at the 2017 Glastonbury Festival; they defined "fuckboy".

> " A LOT OF PEOPLE SEEM TO THINK I'M A KIND OF BRITISH JUSTIN BIEBER AND IT'S ONLY GIRLS THAT ARE INTO ME, BUT IT'S REALLY A 50/50 THING. "

ED SHEERAN

had identified a particular kind of male loser – the "basic" guy who aspires to hipness, assiduously wearing the right clothes and doing the right things, but inevitably getting it wrong. This is where Sheeran's ability to use a zoom lens on human behaviour really comes into its own. The new man wears Ed Hardy jeans, has a "tribal" tattoo chosen not for its significance to him but because it's cool, drives a Vauxhall Corsa with a *Ministry of Sound 2001* compilation blaring out and, every time he hears a hip-hop song, fires an imaginary gun and shouts "choooon!" (the weekend raver's annoying pronunciation of "tune"). Those are

only a few of the cheap-but-funny shots taken – there are a dozen more digs, including the man bag, the plucked eyebrows, the anal bleaching. If all that weren't enough, the poor sucker wears sunglasses indoors.

The inspiration for that last detail came from a rapper Sheeran met at a soundcheck early in his career, when both were on the same bill at London's Proud Gallery. The rapper, soundchecking before him, spent 10 minutes fussing over the microphone sound level, which was eight minutes too long, cutting into Sheeran's soundcheck time. And, of course, he was wearing shades indoors. When the time came to do a

"fuckboy anthem", the rapper came to mind (the only other thing he remembered about that night was that the flyer for the gig spelled his name Sheermington).

This "fuckboy" specimen, he told Zane Lowe, is usually the first guy a woman dates after she ends a long-term relationship: "I don't mean the guy she ends up in a relationship with, the first guy she gets with." Most reviewers saw the wit in it, though there was the odd one, such as *Vulture's* Craig Jenkins, who discerned only "absurd details" and "corny pettiness". Yet he let pass without comment what you might call the song's darker side, where Sheeran turns his attention to the ex-girlfriend. If the "new man" is a work of fiction, it's not entirely certain that the girlfriend is. In the song, the narrator is dismayed by the way she's changed since taking up with the new boyfriend. She used to sit next to the river, dreamily reading books, but now she's gone basic – spending hours in the gym, stuffing kale down her throat and idolising the Kardashians. The narrator knows this because he's been "creeping" her Instagram, scrolling all the way down to look at her earliest posts and trying to refrain from "liking" them because it would reveal that he'd been there.

The narrator knows she doesn't love the new man because he spotted her kissing another guy; not only that, she's been ringing him – the ex-boyfriend – for ambiguous chats. Emboldened, he steps in and offers his services. She must be lonely, he tells her, so why doesn't she come back to him, given that she obviously misses him? The new guy can't give her the love she craves so there's no need to be with him. If she wants to resume her old relationship, the protagonist's door is always open.

On one level, this is Sheeran all over. Much of his songwriting persona is founded on wistfulness – he's the guy who's always a little mopey about the one that got away. "New Man" is all about wistfulness. The girl in the lyrics was very much his kind of girl – unflashy, a bit homespun, happy to spend a couple of hours reading on the riverbank (let's assume, for romance's sake, that it was his local river, the Orwell, which flows through the entire county of Suffolk). Thus, he's crushed and the disappointment makes him waspishly critical of the new boyfriend.

Lyrically speaking, he's often at his most charming when lovelorn but the self he reveals on "New Man" is less sweet. For once, Sheeran – or whoever the storyteller is meant to be – seems patronising and a bit entitled. It's a song of two halves: first come the hilarious diss segments, then follows the rest of it. In the second half, the protagonist starts off with misty memories – that time they drank champagne by funnelling it into cider cans, for example. But, after that, he becomes petulant, chiding her for phoning him and then pinning her down with, "Right, no more about the new bloke – let's focus on your life, love." That's when he disdainfully lists the changes in her: kale, gym and all the rest. It's not Sheeran's finest hour.

Perhaps, after the initial thrill of writing it had passed, even he was ambivalent about it. When Asylum insisted that it go onto the standard edition of ÷, he was unwilling. He considered ÷ his "definitive album", telling the *Guardian* that he'd be overjoyed if it had the same resonance for future artists that Damien Rice's *O* had for him. "I'd love for some kid who in 20 years' time is a huge artist to be, like, 'Wow, that album.'"

In short, he didn't want what he regarded as a light-hearted bonus track to appear among the 12 standard-version tracks, where its references to anal bleaching and choooons would vie for attention with the serious songcraft of "Perfect" and "Happier". If he could have swapped its place in the track-listing with the bonus number "Save Myself", he would have ("Save Myself", the final song of the deluxe edition, is discussed later, but he considered it "classic"). In terms of fan approval, though, it's one of ÷'s biggest songs. In the week that every track on the album entered the UK Top 20, "New Man" perched at Number 5, eventually selling over 400,000 copies.

OPPOSITE: Slightly dishevelled at the premiere for the "Jumpers for Goalposts" concert film, in October 2015. What would his "new man" nemesis say?

OVERLEAF: Playing to a packed Air Canada Centre on the first of two nights in Toronto, July 2017.

HEARTS DON'T BREAK AROUND HERE

The River Orwell gets namechecked on this pretty ballad, which Sheeran wrote at his kitchen table. It's his favourite song on the record, perhaps because it captures both his deep love for his home county's countryside and his feelings for Cherry Seaborn, who is from the same landscape. It also has special significance because it's one of the songs that he produced alone. Having tested the water and found it "fun" to make all the decisions about which noise should go where, Ed intends to produce his entire next album alone.

As with most major pop albums of the 2010s, ÷'s production was overseen by a cast of big-name operatives. Along with old compadres Benny Blanco and Johnny McDaid, he worked with Steve Mac, Will Hicks (who was Grammy nominated for his work on x), Mike Elizondo and Labrinth. Despite all the disparate voices, ÷ consistently felt like the work of one man: Sheeran himself. Scant surprise, then, that he intends to go it alone for album four, which he began working on shortly after ÷'s release. It may also have crossed his mind that no outside producers meant no production royalties based on sales.

"I DON'T REALLY DO THAT WHOLE 'SINGLE LIFE' THING."

ED SHEERAN

ABOVE: Cherry Seaborn leaving the "Jumpers for Goalposts" after-party in London, October 2015.

OPPOSITE: Will Hicks at Cobnash Recording Studio in Herefordshire. He was nominated for a 2015 Grammy for his engineering work on x.

Interestingly, he foresees a lower level of success for the fourth album. "The next album, I promise you, will sell less, but this album [÷] will sell more [than x]. I don't think I'll have a year like this again," he told the *Guardian*. His astuteness does him credit. Even in the middle of a year in which he broke every chart record, he understood that 2017 might be his commercial peak and was already anticipating fewer sales next time, which will inevitably precipitate "Is Ed Sheeran finished?" stories.

He predicted that "Hearts Don't Break" would be the Sheerios' favourite ÷ song. Its tender evocation of home, and of Cherry, make it the stuff of fans' dreams. It also has the attraction of being tucked away in the second half of the album – what would be the B-side, were it released on vinyl (it was but on a small, completists-only scale). It lacks the obvious, big-ticket bang of "Shape of You" and "Castle on the Hill", appealing more to the connoisseur who had gravitated towards the similarly scaled-down "Kiss Me" and "Tenerife Sea" on the previous albums. Sheeran had actually written "Hearts Don't Break" with those songs in mind, after noticing that what ÷ lacked was a similarly unassuming romantic tune.

That was his producer brain at work. Before starting studio sessions, he knew exactly what genres ÷ would contain – from folk to rap to Gaelic – and wrote at least 10 songs for each category, with the best one of each making it onto the record. As a music fan, he also understood fan psychology. True believers tend to prefer lesser-known tracks to the giant hits: if even your grandmother knows every word of "Shape of You", that eradicates any coolness it may have had. Although Ed occasionally played "Hearts Don't Break Around Here" on the 186-date tour that took up most of his 2017 and 2018, it remains one of his least-heard songs.

His warm voice lightly picks through the track, underpinned by a folkish, guitar-based arrangement. Apart from synths and piano, he plays nearly every instrument, including "body percussion" – the practice of slapping legs and chest to achieve a unique sound. The lyrics radiate contentment.

His life with Cherry in the pastoral countryside is described in pretty verses that rank as his most unguarded declarations of love. A couplet that rhymes "soul" with "pothole" is excusable in the face of so much emotion: she's his light; the one who makes him unafraid of getting old. She's the Orwell itself, flowing through his life, and Sheeran, who's experienced a remarkable amount of romantic turmoil for a young man, feels so secure with her that he can confidently say, "Hearts don't break around here."

WHAT DO I KNOW?

Having quietly supported half a dozen charities for some time, Sheeran was awarded an MBE for services to music and charity in the 2017 Queen's Birthday Honours. He's helped raise thousands of pounds for East Anglia's Children's Hospices, the Elton John AIDS Foundation and a number of others, but his efforts for Comic Relief are the most visible of his good works. In March 2017, he teamed up with DJs from the West London pirate radio station Kurupt FM (who are the subject of the BBC3 series *People Just Do Nothing*) to make a Kurupt-style garage version of the album track "What Do I Know?"

The encounter was filmed and included highlights such as entrepreneur Chabuddy G telling the rest of the crew that they were about to meet "one of the biggest urban artists in the world," followed by crushed hopes when they discovered it wasn't Stormzy. Sheerer (as Chabuddy misnomers him) is mistaken for the tea boy, then told his song needs a lot of work to bring it up to Kurupt's standards. Frankly, they explain to Sheerer, it's "shit".

The trouble with the track, the fictitious DJs go on to say, is that it doesn't have enough of a message. Instead of crooning about changing the world with love, why doesn't Sheeran say that garage can change the world? "This song, yeah, is about bringing garage to Africa," says Kurupt's DJ Steves. "I don't know if the continent of Africa knows or cares about garage," Sheeran rejoinders. "Well, maybe that's part of the problem then, Ed," snaps DJ Beats. Happily, they resolve their differences and write a banger of a garage remix, credited to "Kurupt FM x Ed Sheeran".

BELOW: The Kurupt FM crew enjoying a takeaway from the hip hop world's favourite eatery, Nando's at Parklife Festival, Manchester, June 2017.

OPPOSITE: Starburst lighting during Ed's set on the Pyramid stage at Glastonbury on 25 June 2017.

If any ÷ song offered itself up for parody, it was "What Do I Know?" because it was that Ed rarity, an overtly political track delivered with maximum earnestness. It wouldn't even have existed, he told *People* magazine, if he hadn't been trying to impress the head of Asylum Records. He'd come to Sheeran's place in Suffolk for the day and the singer, who'd already started writing the track, decided to wow him with how quickly he could finish it. He dashed it off there and then, reflecting later that its provenance made it "quite a weird one."

At least he knew what he was getting into: the song opens with him musing that his father had warned him never to talk publicly about politics or religion. The lyrics make it clear that he's uncertain about whether it's a good idea to share his sentiments as he is about to. He feels so unqualified to express a political opinion that his doubts surface repeatedly through the song. "What do I know?" he asks six times. (In an interview, he elaborated, "[I'm] 25-year-old Ed from Suffolk who doesn't read newspapers. Like, 'What do you know, mate?'") Yet, appalled at the inequality and injustice that he has witnessed, he's compelled to have his say. He has the platform of fame and the medium of music, an international language, so he decides that it's worth a go.

There is a utopian naïveté to the lyrics, though, and a few plunges into cliché. Sheeran contends, for instance, that too many of us are only interested in making money and being skinny enough to wear the right jeans – an observation that's not new to anybody who's looked around them in the past 50 years. Never mind, these people will probably be the first up against the wall, come the "revolution" that Sheeran predicts is imminent. He'll be doing his bit, singing his song and sharing the love that was showered on him by his family, which he will, in turn, pass to his own future children.

"YOU CAN'T SELL 22 MILLION ALBUMS, THEN READ A REVIEW BY ONE PERSON AND BE LIKE: 'NO-ONE LIKES ME.'"

ED SHEERAN

Anyone who fails to detect the fundamental sweetness and concern is doing the singer a disservice. Love is the fulcrum of Sheeran's existence and the filter through which he views many things, including politics. Even so, he was probably wise to add the "What do I know?" disclaimer. If anyone picked on him for claiming that complex problems can be solved by everyone picking up a guitar – and some reviewers did pick on him – he can at least say that he hadn't claimed to be an expert. For good measure, the song mentions that he hasn't been to university – the fourth tune of his to say so. This time, though, there's no chip-on-shoulder. He's just saying that anyone can make a difference, university degree or not.

The essence of the song is his innate modesty battling with the desire to say something big. Whatever the tune's flaws, his modesty is far more attractive than the opposite condition, the urge to pontificate. In an interview, though, Sheeran mused that pontificators such as Bono have gravitas, which young Ed from Suffolk doesn't. He may have enough celebrity currency to be allowed the use of Damien Hirst's "spinner" to paint ÷'s cover art but lacks the weightiness that makes Bono rock's chief humanitarian haranguer. Indeed, the song's final words pose the same question: "What do I know?"

Apart from employing the services of drum programmer Joe Rubel, Sheeran played every instrument here. Consequently, it has a rustic warmth that's closer to country than to pop. Strumming what sounds like a banjo – actually his Little Martin guitar – Sheeran is relaxed, delivering his State of the Union address as if he were slouching on the back porch of a clapboard house in Tennessee. There's some background humming that's incongruously similar to that on "Bloodstream" but adds texture to the otherwise unadorned arrangement. Despite Sheeran's (and Kurupt's) reservations, "What Do I Know?" is brave and enjoyable.

PREVIOUS, OPPOSITE, AND ABOVE: Closing the Glastonbury Festival, 25 June 2017.

HOW WOULD YOU FEEL (PAEAN)

"How Would You Feel (Paean)" comes out tomorrow at midnight wherever you are in the world, its not the next single, but is one of my favzzzzz," tweeted Sheeran in February 2017.

The song that follows "What Do I Know?" finds Sheeran back on less knotty turf. The "paean" was written very early in his relationship with Cherry, dating it to around summer 2015 (which coincided with Sheeran topping a Spotify poll of the 25 most influential artists under the age of 25, based on total streams, Number 1 hits and growth of streams). She'd been working in New York for three years when Sheeran arrived in the city to play shows, and a mutual friend who was working on his tour arranged Sheeran and Cherry to reconnect. Not long afterwards, she returned to Framlingham for a local festival, where they suddenly saw each other in a much more interesting light. He hasn't revealed which festival but the time frame of their relationship suggests that it could have been the Framlingham Country Show & Festival of Dogs, which offered not just dogs but rural crafts, local food and a stage with eight bands playing each day.

When Cherry left to return to New York, Sheeran, sitting at home, decided that her three-hour cab ride to the airport gave him just enough time to pen a tune. "I thought I'd write a song quickly and send it to her so she's got something to listen to on the drive, and then forgot about it," he told Capital Radio.

Still basking in the afterglow of her visit, Sheeran composed a wildly romantic piece in which he declared his feelings about her. And if he'd knocked out "What Do I Know?" quickly, he excelled himself with "(Paean)" – it came to him in less than an hour. He recorded it on his iPhone, put it on a memo and sent it to Cherry. Then, goes the story, he forgot about it for the next year. Paean, by the way, is Cherry's middle name.

With Cherry based in New York, their first few months together were conducted long distance and their first real date didn't happen for a couple of

OPPOSITE: Headlining the Pyramid stage on day 3 of the Glastonbury Festival 2017.

BELOW: At the 56th Grammy Awards with friend Taylor Swift, whose 4th of July bash saw Cherry introduced to the world.

months. It finally came about in July 2015, when Sheeran was in Manhattan and took her to a birthday party for Adele's manager. To gauge whether they would be compatible, he set her a test, leaving her to her own devices while he talked to other guests for several hours. For Sheeran, who is constantly pulled away by other guests at social events, self-reliance was a crucial quality in a woman. If she couldn't hack it, she'd find it impossible to date him.

When Ed finally returned, Cherry was engrossed in conversation with someone else and didn't want to leave the party. Satisfied that she had the right stuff, he's been with her ever since and a large proportion of the songs he's written in the past year or two are inspired by or directly about her. The first the world knew of the relationship was on their first anniversary, which coincided with Taylor Swift's annual 4th of July bash. Usually an excuse for Swift and her "squad" of beautiful friends to be photographed frolicking on the beach at her Rhode Island house, she turned the 2016 party into an anniversary celebration.

The song is about getting up the courage to tell his girl he loves her – a big declaration that's always fraught with risk, even when it's obvious that the feeling is mutual. To shore up his position, he reminds her of intimate moments they've shared: kissing in a car, staying up all night to watch the sun rise and walking along the riverbank when the lilacs were in blossom. He considers the romance a potential lifetime proposition and paints an idyllic picture of their present and future life together. He's prepared to let things develop at their own pace; not for Sheeran the celebrity practice of falling in love at the first provocation, then falling out of it just as quickly. As a "loverman", he's in it for the long haul.

This was the first track on ÷ that Sheeran self-produced. It's a particularly personal track for Ed and also one of the album's more pared-back musical arrangements, at least for the first couple of minutes. The full track is nearly five minutes long, which would have ruled it out for most radio playlists but Sheeran was bent on securing airplay because he loved the song. To get around it, he released it as an unofficial single in the fallow period between "Shape of You" in January and the album's 10 March release date. As insurance, he decided to put it out on 17 February, his 26th birthday, gauging that the combination of new song and birthday would impel stations to play it, even at five minutes long.

Slow and stately at first, it flowers from a piano-and-voice ballad into full-bodied luxury involving cello, drums and a John Mayer guitar solo. Apropos Mayer, he was invited to play after Sheeran decided that his own guitar solo was "shit". He'd been trying to emulate Mayer, whose blues-rock skills made him one of Eric Clapton's favourite younger guitarists, before remembering that he had Mayer's email address – they'd performed "Thinking Out Loud" together at the 2015 Grammys – and might as well ask the man himself. The next day, Mayer returned the track with a languid blues solo that starts at around three minutes in and electrifies proceedings.

When Sheeran heard it, he decided that what had been a bare-bones sketch was now a proper song. Mayer, for his part, seemed tickled to have been asked to contribute. The day it came out as a non-single single, he tweeted, "when I played the solo on new track, I also sent another take played 1/2 step down [using different tuning], just to confuse his engineer." (Evidently not spotting Mayer's name in the credits, *Billboard* praised Sheeran for his "Mayer-esque" solo.)

Sheeran could have flagged up Mayer's presence by adding a "featuring John Mayer" to the track-list, which would have prompted the guitarist's own fanbase to investigate the song. He decided that it was far cooler not to draw attention to it. What he had first intended was to create a Van Morrison-ish, white-soul anthem and it does, in fact, induce thoughts of Morrison's "Have I Told You Lately". However, even with Mayer's distinctive solo, the finished item is unmistakably Ed.

Sheeran would never have remembered "How Would You Feel (Paean)" had he not played the nearly finished LP to Cherry and asked her which song she liked most. Her favourite, she replied, wasn't even on the album because he'd sent her the only copy in existence, then forgotten about it. At that point, she was the only person who had even heard it. She emailed it to him and he hastily recorded it and added it to the album. There was talk of making it a bonus track but it got into the main line-up – "a one-hundred percenter," he called it, and manager Stuart Camp agreed, predicting that it would be bigger than "Perfect".

OPPOSITE: Sheeran and Cherry getting into the baseball spirit during a game between the Philadelphia Phillies and New York Mets at Citi Field in New York, 2 September 2015.

OVERLEAF: Sheeran and John Mayer dressed up for the 57th Grammy Awards.

"I THINK 2017 IS GOING TO BE THE HIGH POINT. I HAVE A FEELING ABOUT IT. SEVENTEEN IS MY LUCKY NUMBER."

ED SHEERAN

SUPERMARKET FLOWERS

Fittingly, the last song on ÷ is the one Sheeran deems "the most special" on the album. He had written several times about his paternal grandparents, William and Anne Sheeran ("Afire Love", "Nancy Mulligan"), but never about his mother's parents, Stephen and Shirley Lock. Shirley was a singer who had performed for Benjamin Britten and Imogen Holst (Sheeran's mother, Imogen, was named after her), and was a member of several nationally renowned choirs, including the Ambrosian Singers and Purcell Singers; Stephen Lock CBE was a doctor who became a medical journalist, and was a former editor of the *British Medical Journal*.

When the album's song titles were first revealed, in January 2017, "Supermarket Flowers" incited a multitude of tweets accusing Sheeran of being such a tightwad that he bought supermarket flowers for his girlfriend. The lyrics put paid to that misconception.

The song was set in a hospital room, which Sheeran was clearing out after Shirley's death. There's poetry in the finely wrought observations: the cup of undrunk tea, an album of photos made by his brother, Matthew, his grandmother's nightdresses packed away in an overnight bag. The supermarket flowers were in a vase on the windowsill, forgotten.

There was a misconception there too: because the lyrics are written in the first person, the assumption is that the protagonist is Sheeran. While he was indeed present in the room, it's his mother whose viewpoint

ABOVE: British composer Imogen Holst (1907-1984) conducting a string section at Oxford Church, Suffolk, circa 1950. Sheeran's mother was named after her.

OPPOSITE: Visiting SiriusXM studios in New York with Jamie Lawson, the first signing to Sheeran's Gingerbread Man Records, 29 September 2015.

" I WROTE 'SUPERMARKET FLOWERS' THE DAY MY GRAN PASSED AWAY. YOU CAN BE REALLY UPSET AND DWELL ON SOMETHING OR YOU CAN PUT ALL THE GOOD MEMORIES IN ONE SONG. "

ED SHEERAN

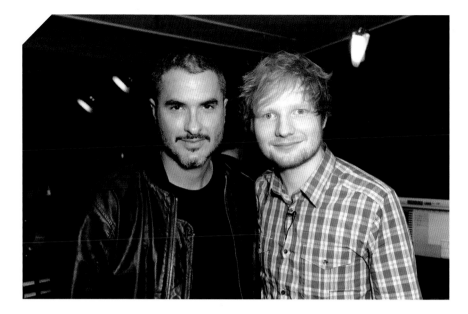

OPPOSITE: A very baby-faced Sheeran with his family, parents Imogen and John Sheeran, and brother Matthew Sheeran in 2011.

RIGHT: Future Beats 1 presenter Zane Lowe (then of Radio 1) and Sheeran at the Beats Present: Sound Symposium in London on 10 July 2014.

is represented here, as she numbly makes the hospital bed and tidies the room, trying to comfort herself with the thought that her own mother had lived a long, productive life. Knowing that Shirley will be welcomed by God when she arrives in Paradise sustains her but she is unseated by the mundanity of her task, crying as she sweeps away the get-well cards.

Fittingly, it's pared back to nothing more than Sheeran's voice, with its occasional cracks, a piano and the distant sound of a keyboard-produced choir. He said he wrote it with the intention of making people weep and, judging from the online response, they did. Even Zane Lowe, the former Radio 1 evening-show presenter turned Beats 1 DJ, told Sheeran that the track couldn't be a single because the content was just "too much [to take]." Lowe, who invented the influential feature Hottest Record in the World Right Now while on Radio 1 was a Sheeran supporter from way back. Sheeran nabbed the Hottest Record slot a few times and gave Lowe one of the first interviews of the ÷ promotional campaign.

While making ÷ at his home recording facility, which he'd named Gingerbread Man Studios (he also launched Gingerbread Man Records in 2015 and had an immediate hit with Jamie Lawson's "Wasn't Expecting That"), he saw Shirley daily. The hospital was nearby and it was there that she died, aged 86, in August 2016. Her grandson was in his studio and, when the news

reached him, he instinctively reached for his guitar and began writing.

He'd kept her updated on the progress of the album and, at her behest, had invited his brother to arrange ÷'s string parts – the first time he and Matthew had worked together. Thus, it seemed fitting to write a song in her memory, although, to spare his grandfather's feelings, he had no intention of putting it on the record. His father encouraged him to play it at Shirley's funeral, where his grandfather, hearing it for the first time, told him it had to be on ÷. Songs about death often use broad-brush profundities but what makes "Supermarket Flowers" work is its smallness. The beautifully observed lines about his mother weeping over the greeting cards and ginger beer are among Sheeran's finest.

Focusing on the minutiae made it an easy write. Had he been set on turning "Supermarket Flowers" into a sweeping statement, the songwriting process would have been considerably more convoluted; even so, it bears a trace of ethereal grandeur. The chorus about angels and what awaits the departed one in the hereafter sounds as if it were intended for a much bigger song, especially against the tininess of the rest. Yet it all hangs together. Sheeran felt that memorialising his grandmother in song was the best way to remember her, musing that it would be nice if his own grandkids do the same when he himself goes.

BARCELONA

The first of ÷'s four bonus tracks, "Barcelona", is several things at once. It's the album's other dance track, after "Shape of You", and shares its tropical accent. It's a throwback to the holiday novelty song – a genre that has petered out in the UK but used to produce one big, Mediterranean-flavoured hit per year. And it's an Englishman's salute to things Iberian. In that respect, all manner of Spanish exotica gets a mention, from sangria and Las Ramblas to La Sagradia Familia and tantalising "mamacitas".

The Brit-abroad aspect is the most bemusing thing about "Barcelona". The equivalent would be a Spanish songwriter swooning over Big Ben, ale and pink-cheeked English roses. Considering that Sheeran travels constantly and is more sophisticated than many, this is a curiously one-dimensional portrait of Barcelona. Considering, too, that he can turn his hand with equal verve to UK pop, Irish traditional and Afrobeats (see "Bibia Be Ye Ye", below), he really misses a beat here.

He and co-producer Benny Blanco have cooked up a melange that's part tourist-fandango and part Ed-from-Suffolk transplanting his romantic self to the land of vino tinto – same guy, warmer weather. There's

a Spanish-language segment consisting of words linked together in no particular order, owing to Sheeran not speaking much Spanish – let alone Catalan, the regional language. He explained that he simply put together the words and phrases he did know, such as "viva la vida", a handy catchphrase that also did duty as a Coldplay album title.

Does Barcelona deserve a better tribute than this? Perhaps, but Freddie Mercury and Montserrat Caballé's own magisterial "Barcelona" sets the bar so high that a mere pop song is bound to sound pallid by comparison. To be fair, Sheeran is not trying to make a definitive statement about Catalonia's beloved capital; he's only recounting a night of dancing, flirting and drinking. It's all executed with such good-hearted gusto that it's hard to seriously dislike it. Barcelonans themselves love the tune, to judge by the reaction when he played the Palau Sant Jordi in April 2017. When he sang the Spanish verse, 17,000 people sang with him, roaring, "Solamente! Mamacita!"

Musically, he throws everything he's got at it, from the opening burst of flamenco guitar and breathy beatboxing, to a jaunty trumpet-and-saxophone interlude (played by Nico Segal and Ian Hendrickson-Smith, respectively). It ranks among his most upbeat moments and there's enough self-deprecation in the first verse to really get the Ed party started: he confesses that he can't dance, but there's wine, a bassline and a pretty girl, so he's winning at life.

It was one of a cluster of songs written with Johnny McDaid in January 2016, when the Snow Patrol guitarist moved to Sheeran's patch of west London. They met every day and worked in McDaid's garden studio, with its outdoor microphone. It was literally outdoors – Sheeran has spoken of birdsong being audible on the first recording of "Barcelona".

Amy Wadge, Benny Blanco and Northern Irish writer/singer Foy Vance, who'd recently signed a deal with Sheeran's Gingerbread Man label, also contributed to the writing.

OPPOSITE: The Gracia Street Festival at night in Barcelona.

ABOVE: Freddie Mercury and Montserrat Caballé perform their own "Barcelona" at the KU club, Ibiza on 29 May 1987.

"THERE'S ONE LINE WHERE I SAY 'SIEMPRE VIVRE LA BARCELONA,' WHICH IS ACTUALLY LATIN, I THINK, BUT IT JUST SOUNDED COOL."

ED SHEERAN

Believe it or not, until halfway through the ÷ recording process, it was earmarked as the first single. If "Shape of You" had existed at that point, it's doubtful that "Barcelona" would have led the pack but, in mid-2016, it looked like the immediate, danceable reintroduction Sheeran needed. There were thoughts of putting it out in September 2016 – just slightly past optimum time for summery singles but not too late to be bought by people returning from Mediterranean holidays. Not only was it a burst of bubbly exuberance but its Spanish rhythm and use of the language showed a different side to the singer.

Sheeran and his team got as far as coming up with a video concept and appointing a director, but were stopped in their tracks by manager Stuart Camp. Ed was told that the album had to be rethought because, as a total piece of work, it wasn't up to scratch.

Rick Rubin had already advised him to write more songs and there were people at the label who were disappointed with what they'd heard so far. With Camp echoing their sentiments, Sheeran was impelled to go back to the drawing board. When he returned with the

LEFT: Performing at the Sports Palace Madrid, 8 April 2017.

record that was finally released, "Shape of You" was picked as the lead single, while "Barcelona" was pushed into the bonus section.

Having to rewrite was a grounding experience. He'd been accustomed to getting his way – prevailing in the disagreement about whether "Galway Girl" should be on the record, for example – but was persuaded that this was one of the times when experience had to trump enthusiasm. As a student of the music industry, Sheeran was a quick learner but lacked the perspective that only comes after decades at the coalface. He bowed to Camp and the others' judgement and went back into the studio. Later, he admitted he was glad he had. After completing the second version, he listened again to the first and perceived the weaknesses that Rubin and the others had heard, musing that, had it been released, it still would have been a hit but not the smash that the final take was.

He allowed that the whole thing had been a lesson in listening to those who had been around longer than he had. There are plenty of artists who have had massive early success and assume that it qualifies them to make every subsequent career decision. They tend to discover that it doesn't, and Sheeran was determined not to let that happen. Piqued as he was at hearing that the record wasn't good enough, he was bent on making it the biggest album of the year, in both sales and artistic terms. A few months' extra work was eminently preferable to being the guy who insisted on doing it his way and had diminishing returns to show for it.

ABOVE: Ian Hendrickson-Smith, who plays the saxophone on "Barcelona", performing with The Loston Harris Quartet at Birdland, New York on 8 July 2014.

BIBIA BE YE YE

Whether it was intended or not, ÷'s bonus section is a travelogue, with three of its four songs spawned by visits to other countries during Sheeran's year off. "Bibia Be Ye Ye" was the boldest step on the album, in so far as it sounded like nothing he'd done before. Part-written in the Ghanaian dialect, Twi, it represented his love of Afrobeats, the poppier and less "conscious" descendant of the West African genre, Afrobeat. His friend Fuse ODG, aka multi-award-winning Ghanaian-British singer Nana Richard Abiona, invited him to visit and he spent three weeks in the country in June 2016. Inevitably, he got a tattoo out of it – an inking of the Ghanaian flag on his stomach – and several songs, composed with Fuse at his ODG Mansion studio.

"Bibia" – Twi for "all will be well" – was the first song they wrote, helped along by the production skills of Joseph "Killbeatz" Addison. Piloted by the highlife guitarist OT, the song buoyantly follows Sheeran through a night of overdoing it that ends with him losing his shoes and being sick on a taxi seat. But bibia be ye ye – it'll be OK in the morning.

"I wanted to be sure he was in it for the right reasons," Fuse told Radio 1Xtra. A superstar in Ghana, Fuse is also a passionate advocate of education and school-building; he lauded Sheeran for "donat[ing] 20K straightaway" to the construction of a new school in Ghana.

For Sheeran, it was a transformative experience. "I visited Ghana last year to make music with Fuse ODG and Killbeatz Addison, and whilst there was exposed to such wonderful culture, food, music and scenery," he explained on Instagram. That was posted on 2 August 2017, when he also announced that there was

now a video to go with the track. The video was an outlier – the song wasn't a single and hadn't even been noticeably hyped up. It was sheer passion for Ghana that was behind it. As in many of Sheeran's videos, he appears only in the last few seconds, turned away from the camera as he gazes at fishing boats in a harbour. The rest of the clip shows the markets, parties and food that had captivated him.

ABOVE: Fuse ODG, who co-wrote "Bibia Be Ye Ye", at the Kendal Calling festival near Penrith, Cumbria in July 2015

"I VISITED GHANA TO MAKE MUSIC WITH FUSE ODG AND KILLBEATZ ADDISION. WHILE THERE I WAS EXPOSED TO SO MUCH WONDERFUL CULTURE AND MUSIC."
ED SHEERAN

NANCY MULLIGAN

"I was angling for this to be a trad [Irish] album," Sheeran told the *Irish Times*. Seven traditional songs were recorded but only two made the cut: "Galway Girl" and this, a capsule version of his paternal grandparents' 62-year marriage. Much against their families' wishes, William Sheeran and Anne (known as Nancy) Mulligan, had a cross-border, mixed-religion romance; he was a Belfast Protestant, she a Catholic from the Republic of Ireland. Ed, one of their 22 grandchildren, sentimentalises their relationship, from the first meeting at Guy's Hospital in London during World War II (he was a dentist, she was a nurse) to the recent past, as they enjoy their golden years in adjoining armchairs.

Couched in a sparky jig played by trad fivesome Beoga, it's drenched in romance; skint and forbidden by Nancy's father to marry, the couple eloped with wedding rings that William made by melting dental gold. "Nancy Mulligan" deserves its place in Sheeran's catalogue by virtue of its subject matter. The story is truly interesting – but, musically, the song feels a little like a trifle.

SAVE MYSELF

The album finishes on a reflective, balladic note. "Save Myself" ended up among the bonus tracks because mentor Elton John told him there were enough slow songs on the standard edition. That makes it seem as if it had been tossed into the long grass, but no – its use as ÷'s finale makes sense.

On first listen, "Save Myself" appears to be a glum sign-off note: singing to a piano and string accompaniment (the latter arranged by Matthew Sheeran), he confesses to feeling tired and used – the very first line rues the fact that he's been giving away his "oxygen" to people who don't deserve it. Then it crystallises into a message song – not something Sheeran often writes but this one is from the heart, and relevant to his primarily female fanbase, who might feel uplifted by its self-empowerment tone.

He finds enough clarity to realise that he has to look after himself before anyone else; the very last line of the last song on ÷ is a reminder that it's impossible to truly love another if self-love is absent.

RIGHT: Guy's Hospital, London, where Sheeran's paternal grandparents, William Sheeran and Nancy Mulligan, met.

OPPOSITE: Niamh Dunne of Beoga performing with her band at the Cambridge Folk Festival, 2017.

OVERLEAF: Onstage at the 18,000-capacity Barclays Center in Brooklyn, New York on 30 September 2017.

SONGS WRITTEN
FOR OTHERS

LOVE YOURSELF – JUSTIN BIEBER

Speaking of loving yourself…

When this was written, during the ÷ studio sessions, the advice to "love yourself" was more pungent – the original line was "fuck yourself". Sheeran and Benny Blanco had Rihanna in mind as the recipient of the song because she had the swagger to be able to utter the F-word without repercussions but they ended up giving it to Bieber. It was the "best-performing" single (taking into account sales, airplay and streaming) of 2016 in America. "It just shows you shouldn't always write stuff off," Sheeran told US radio presenter Carson Daly.

COLD WATER – MAJOR LAZER FEAT. JUSTIN BIEBER AND MØ

The other song that kept Sheeran's name circulating during his gap year was this huge hit, which he can't remember writing. He thinks it dates back to a period of intensive work at Benny Blanco's house but forgot about it until Major Lazer member Diplo emailed to notify him that it was "dope" and that he wanted to record it. Bewildered, Sheeran didn't reply. A second email asked if he minded Justin Bieber singing on it. It eventually dawned on Sheeran that this was one of his Blanco co-writes but his recollection was that it had been much slower than Major Lazer's take. He told Daly, "I remember hearing it and being, like, 'That kind of sounds like me. Oh wait, it was me.'"

MOMENTS – ONE DIRECTION

One Direction were short of songs for their debut album, *Up All Night*, and Sheeran offered this one. "To have it on a multi-platinum album is quite nice," he modestly told Australia's News.com.

BELOW: Sheeran and Justin Bieber attend the premiere of "Ed Sheeran: Jumpers for Goalposts" at the Odeon in London's Leicester Square on 22 October 2015.

I WAS MADE FOR LOVING YOU – TORI KELLY

The only one of his farmed-out songs he wishes he'd saved for himself was this, written for American pop singer Kelly's debut album. He did, at least, manage to duet with her on the track.

EVERYTHING HAS CHANGED – TAYLOR SWIFT

A rare second-division single for Swift (Number 32 in the US), this provoked a spat between Sheeran and Swift when he wanted to use a certain chord and she refused, gesturing at her shelf of Grammys to make her point.

DARK TIMES – THE WEEKND

"The fastest and most talented songwriter I've ever worked with, ever," Abel "The Weeknd" Tesfaye said after he and Sheeran composed this following a party that didn't end till 5am.

STRIP THAT DOWN – LIAM PAYNE

This Top 3 UK hit was a bump-and-grind banger with plenty of the explicitness "Shape of You" only hinted at.

WHEN CHRISTMAS COMES AROUND – MATT TERRY

Released by the winner of the 2016 series of *The X Factor*, this fulfilled Sheeran's longstanding desire to write a hit Christmas song. He intends to release his own festive song at some point but, according to Sheeran's manager, it won't be for a while yet: "That's for the Bublé stage of his career."

BELOW: One Direction at a recording studio in 2014. The boy band did fairly well for themselves after finishing third on the 2010 series of *The X Factor*.

OPPOSITE: With a resplendent Taylor Swift at the 58th Grammy Awards on 15 February 2017.